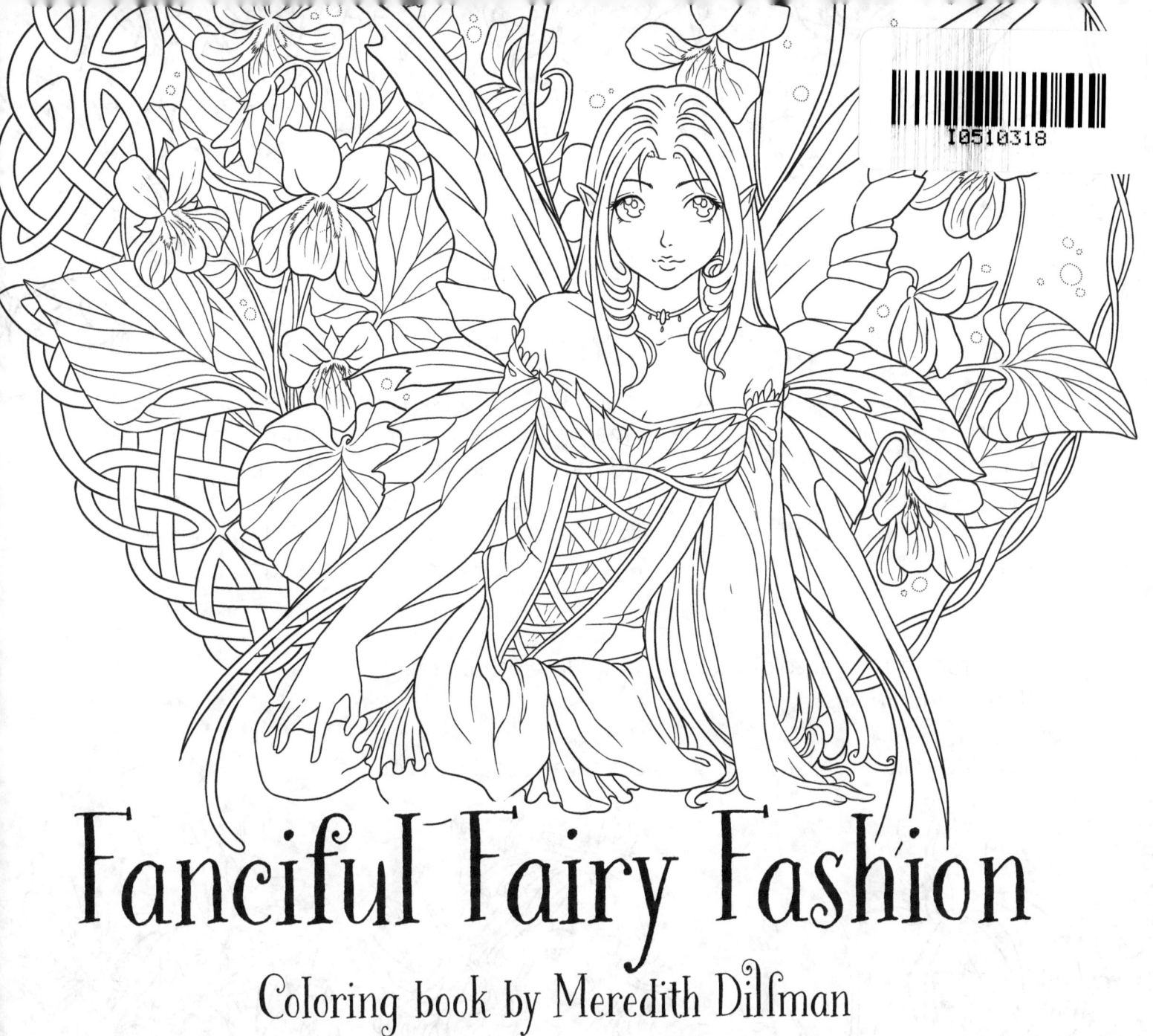

Fanciful Fairy Fashion

Coloring book by Meredith Dillman

This book is a collection of my fairy and fantasy illustrations featuring fantastical women in fantasy fashion with ruffles, ribbons and lace. I have chosen these images from artwork spanning over 10 years of my career (so there are some differences in style over time). Character costumes are inspired by each fairy's place in nature or historical fashion from Victorian, Edwardian and Rococo eras. Each artwork is based one of my finished ink and watercolor paintings. I hope you will enjoy bringing them to life by adding color!

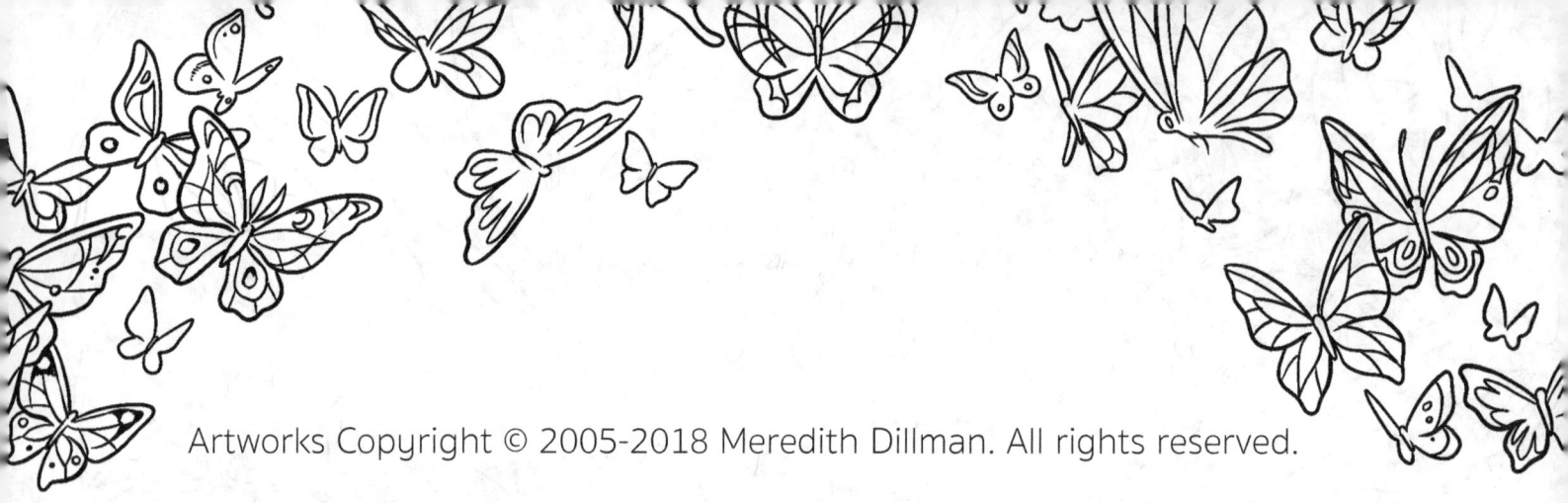

Look for additional coloring books by Meredith Dillman:
"Foxes and Fairies".

Visit Meredith's gallery and shop at meredithdillman.com

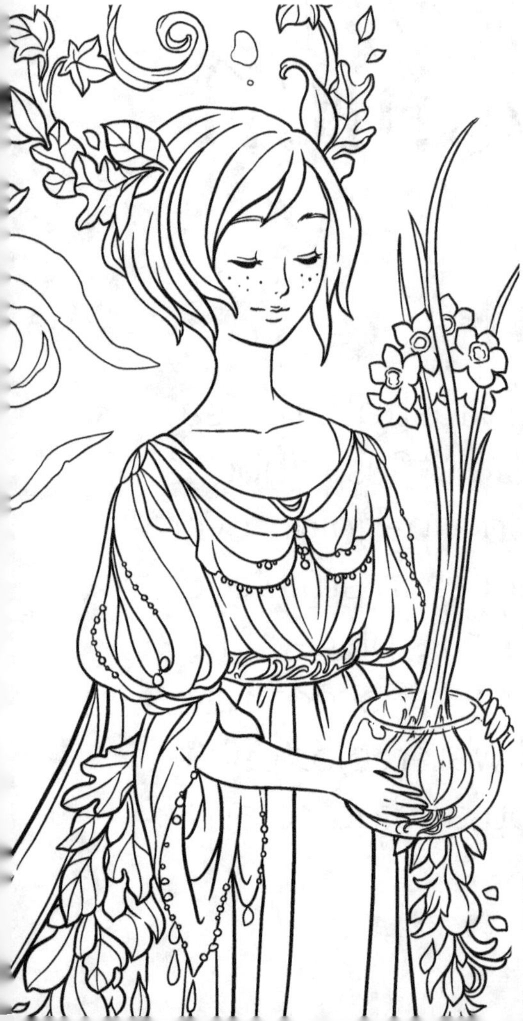

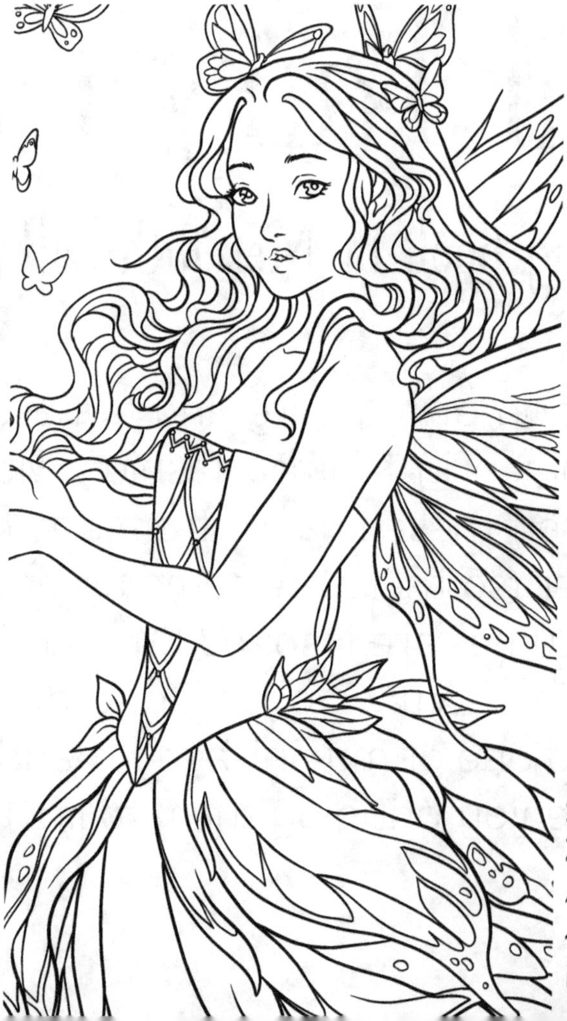

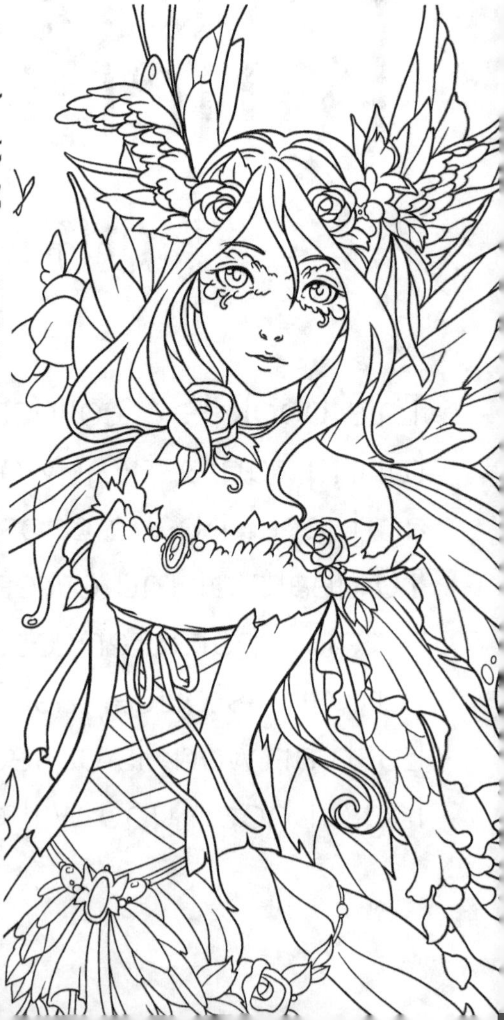

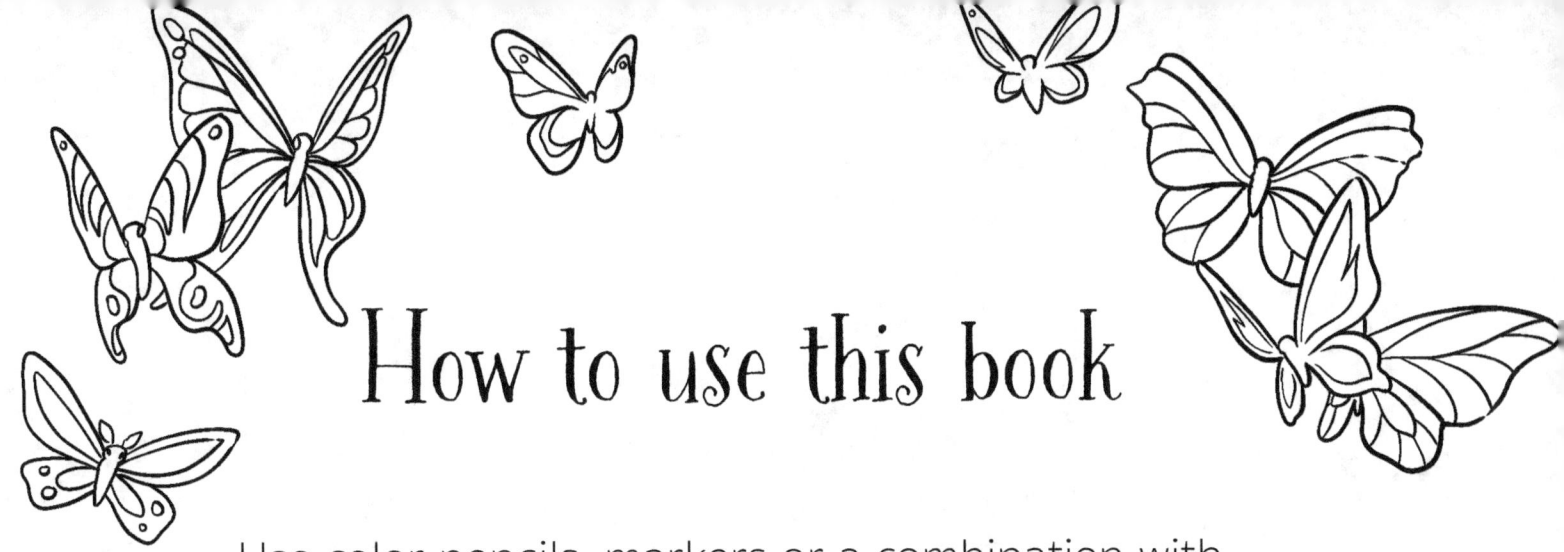

How to use this book

• Use color pencils, markers or a combination with this book. Gel pens and glitter pens make great accents too.

• Images are printed on one side only. The paper is not bleed proof so please place a heavy piece of paper or few sheets of copy paper under each page to avoid bleed through or indentations on other pages.

• Most importantly, have fun and relax! Enjoy bringing each image to life with your own color choices. Remember no color combination is wrong and experimentation is fine. Nothing in art needs to be the color we expect it to be in real life.

• If you post your colored versions online please credit Meredith Dillman and link to meredithdillman.com - Thank you!

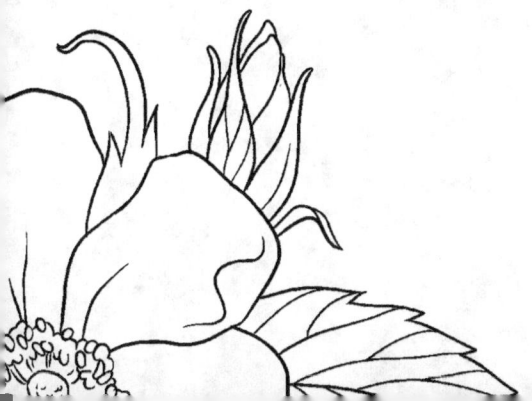

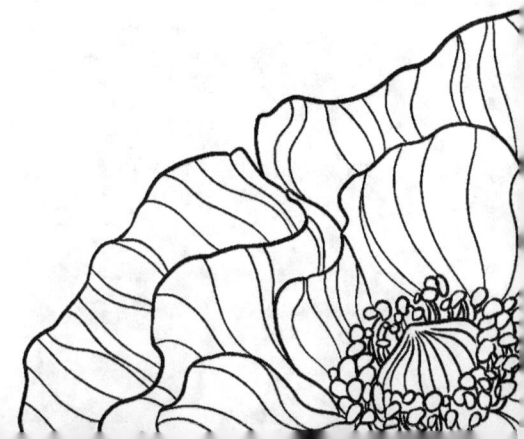

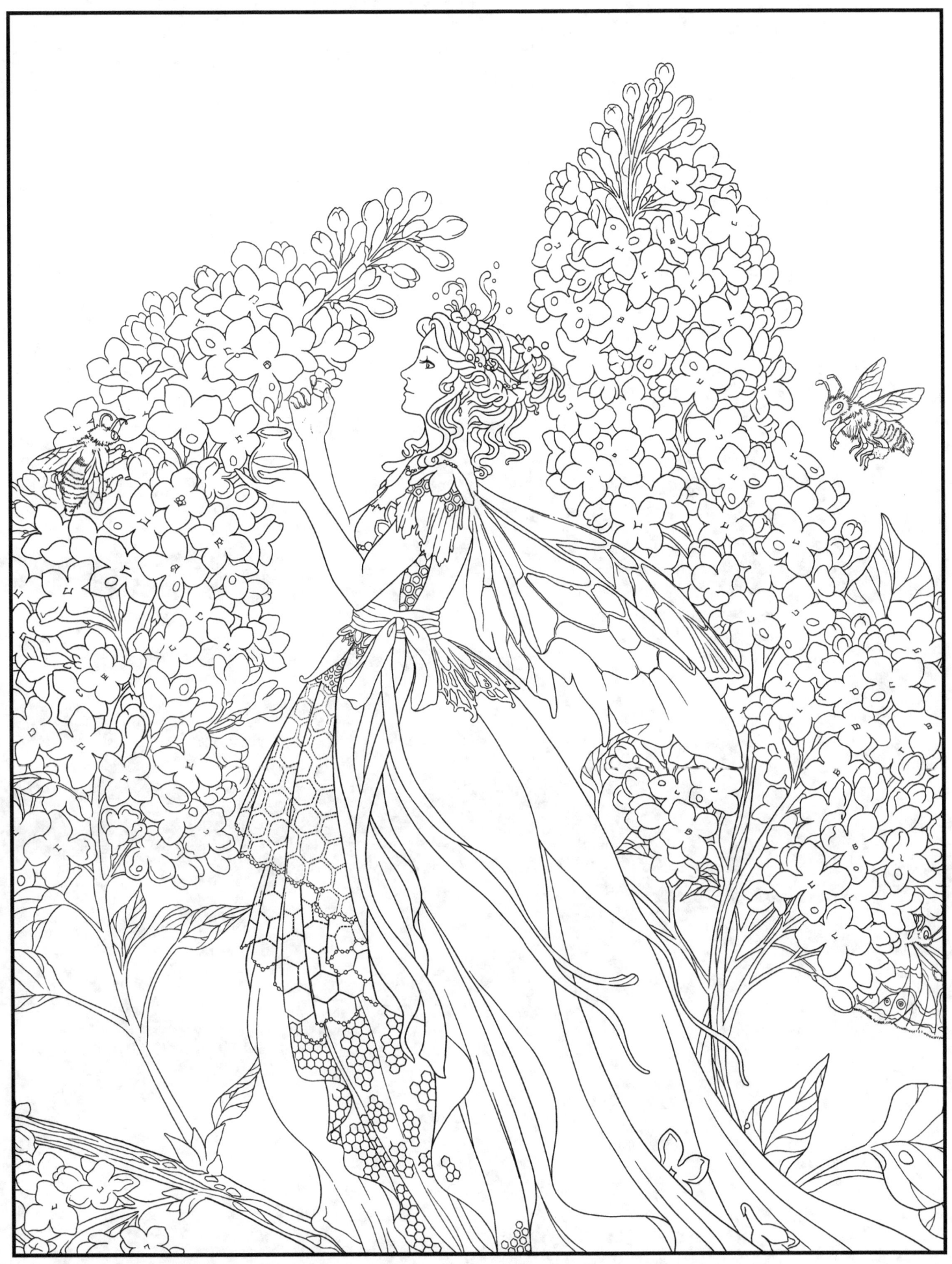

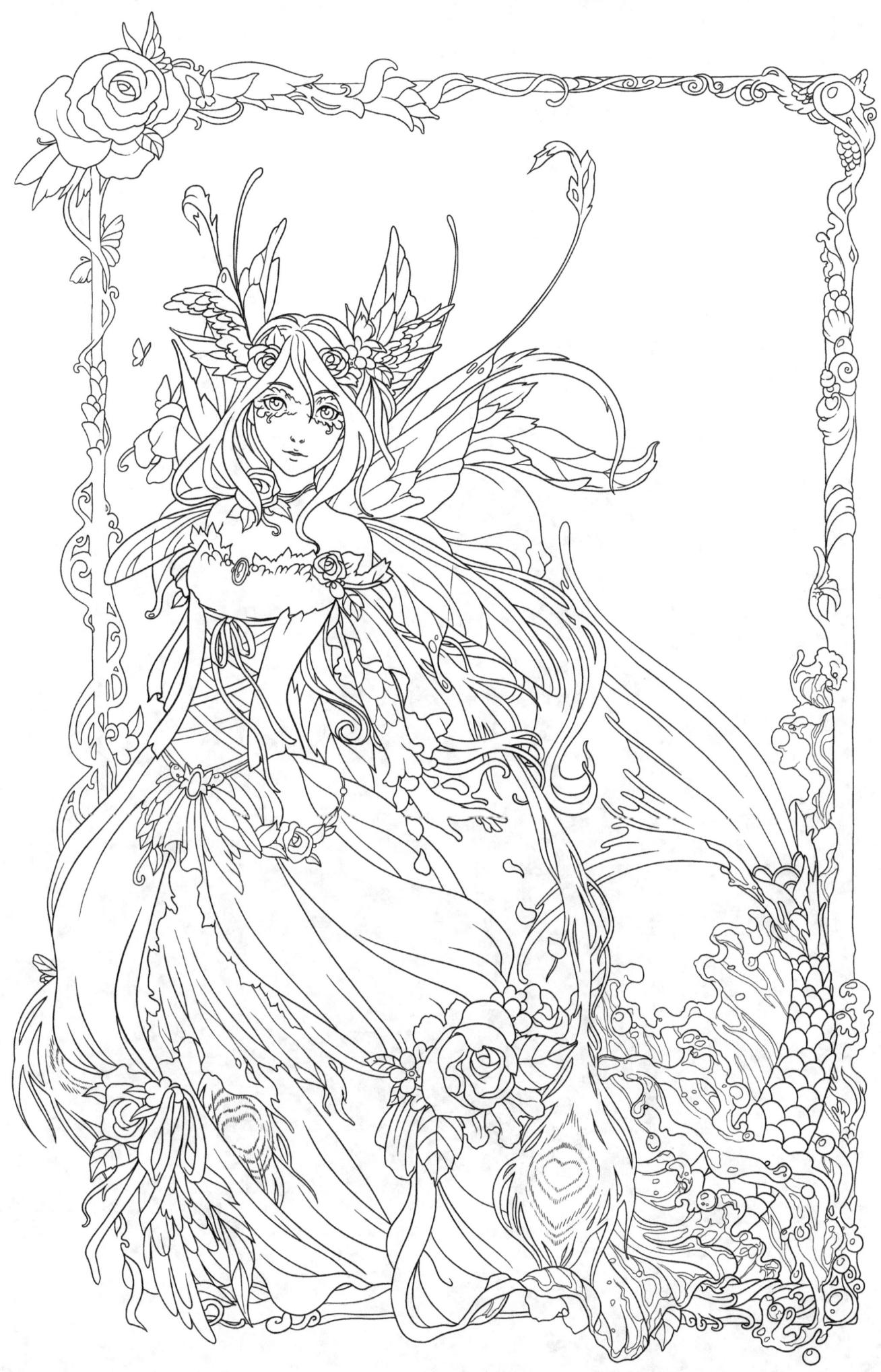

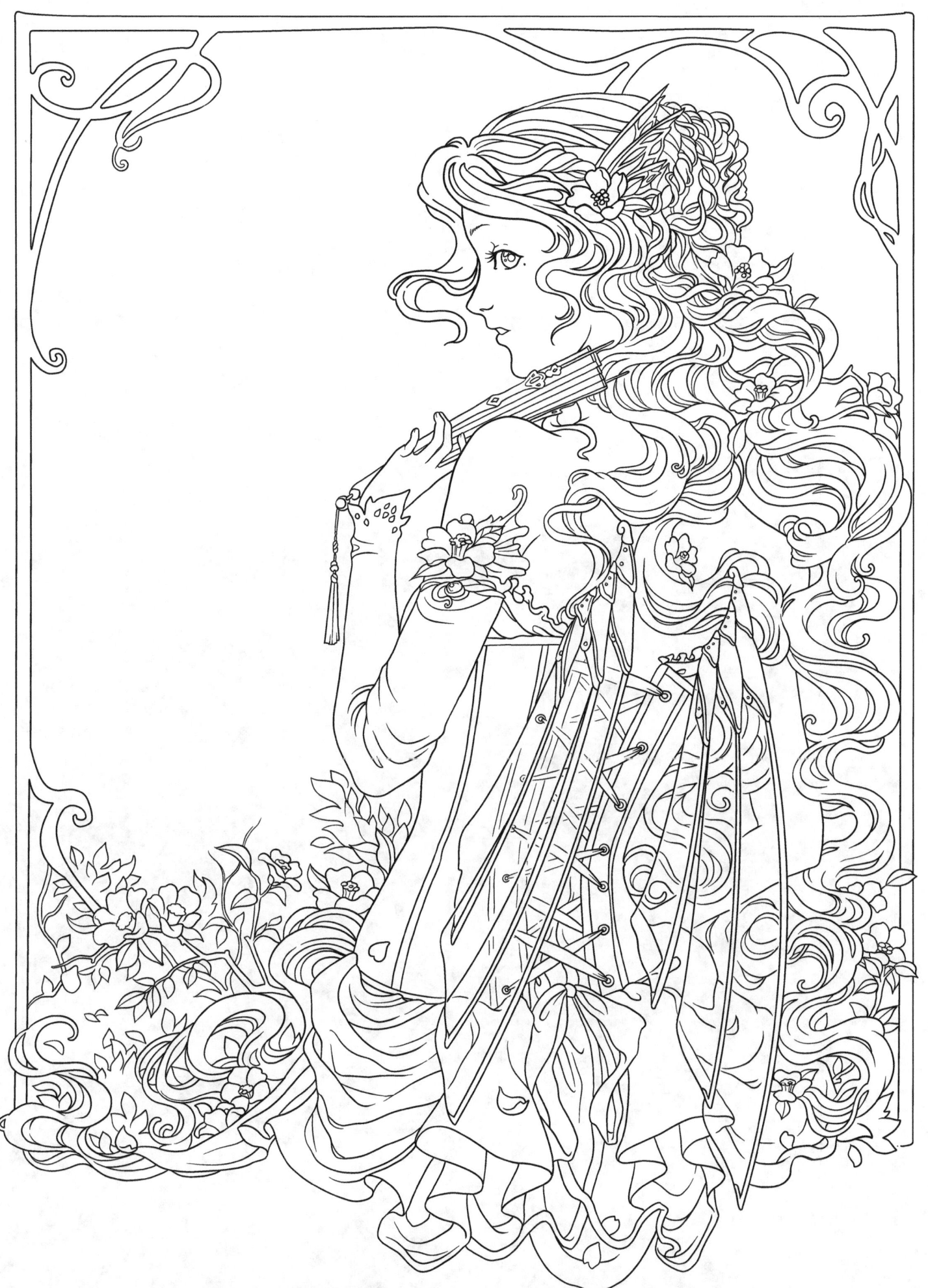

Previous Page: Lady in Green
Lineart by Meredith Dillman

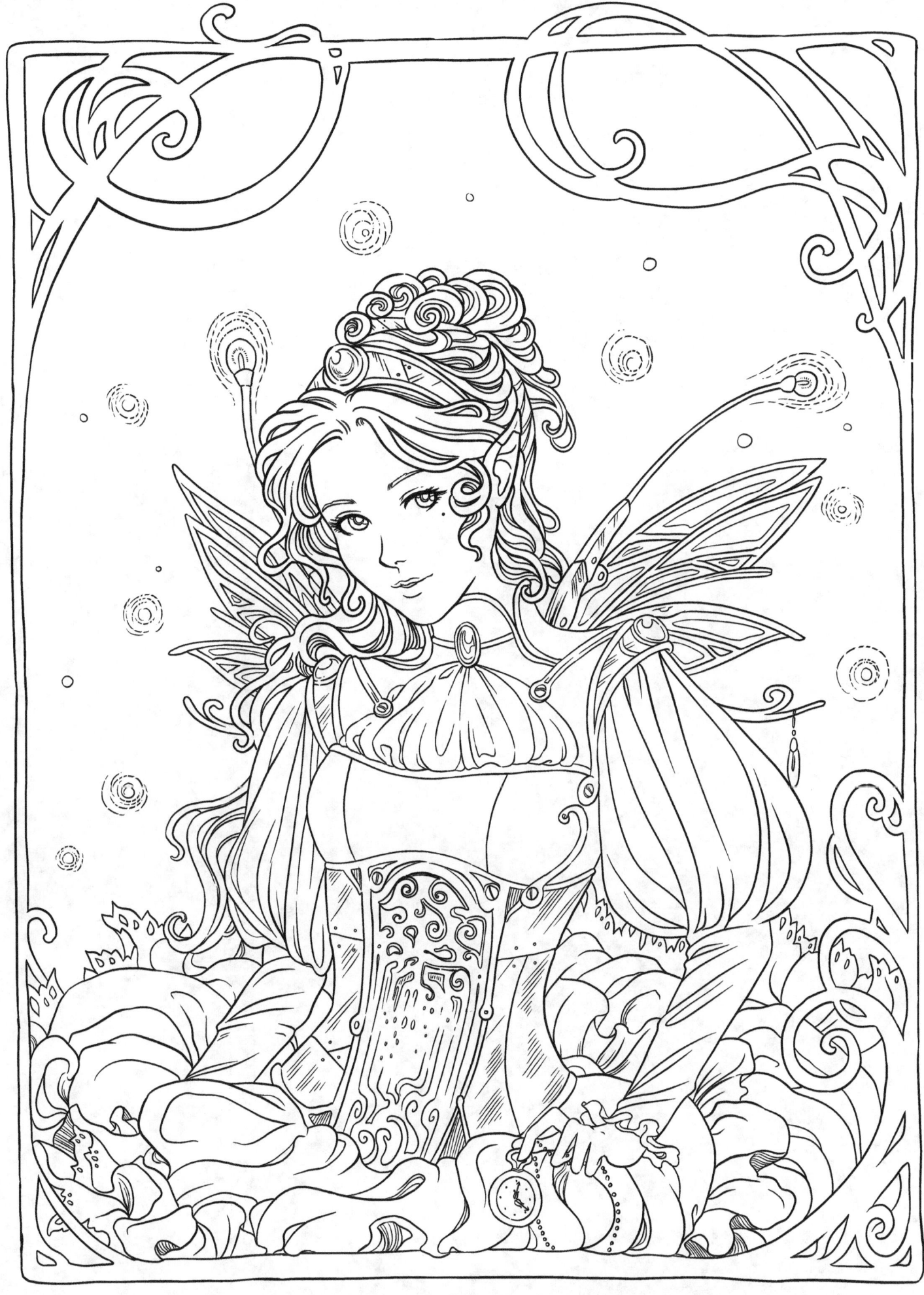

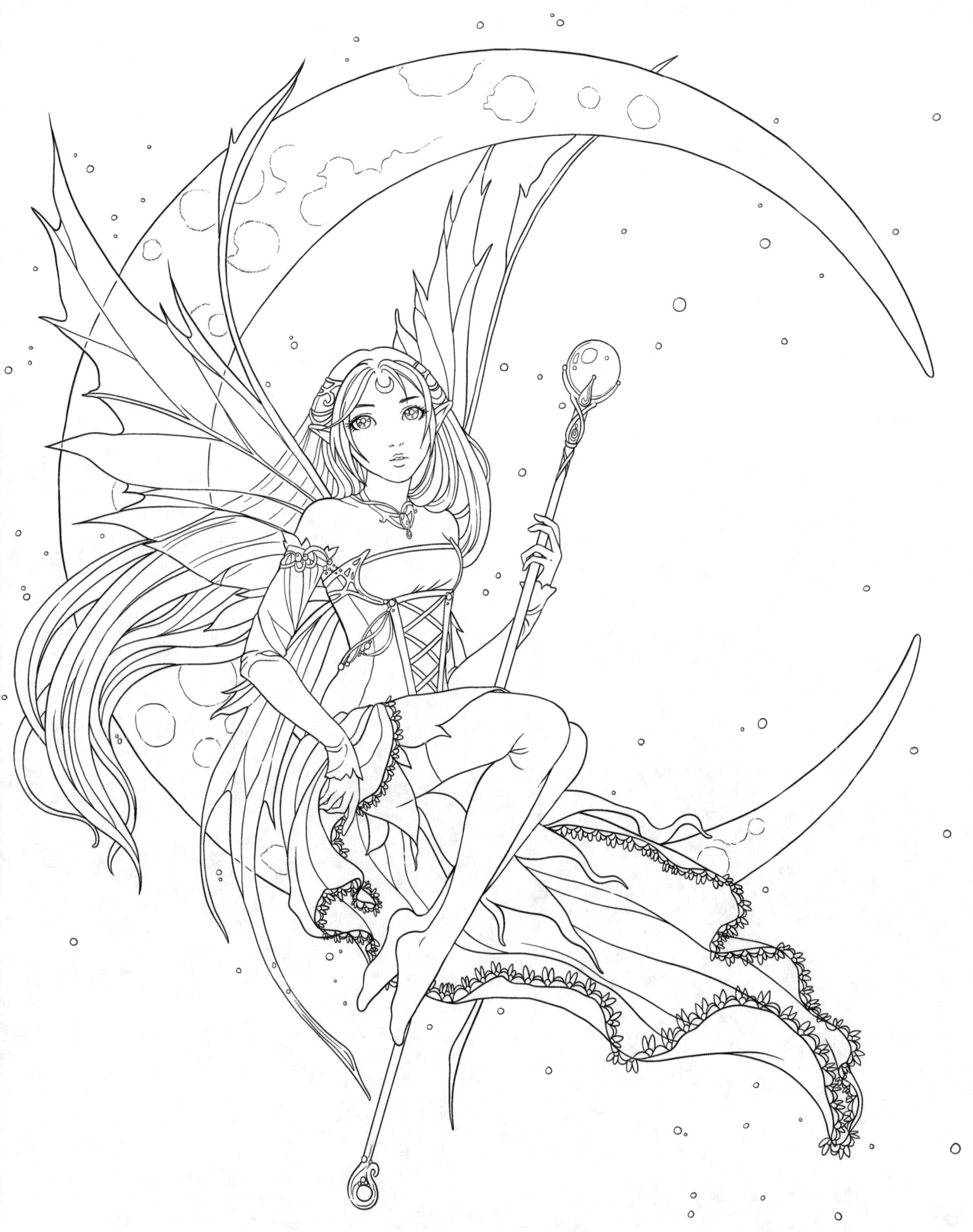

Previous Page: Purple Moon
Lineart by Meredith Dillman

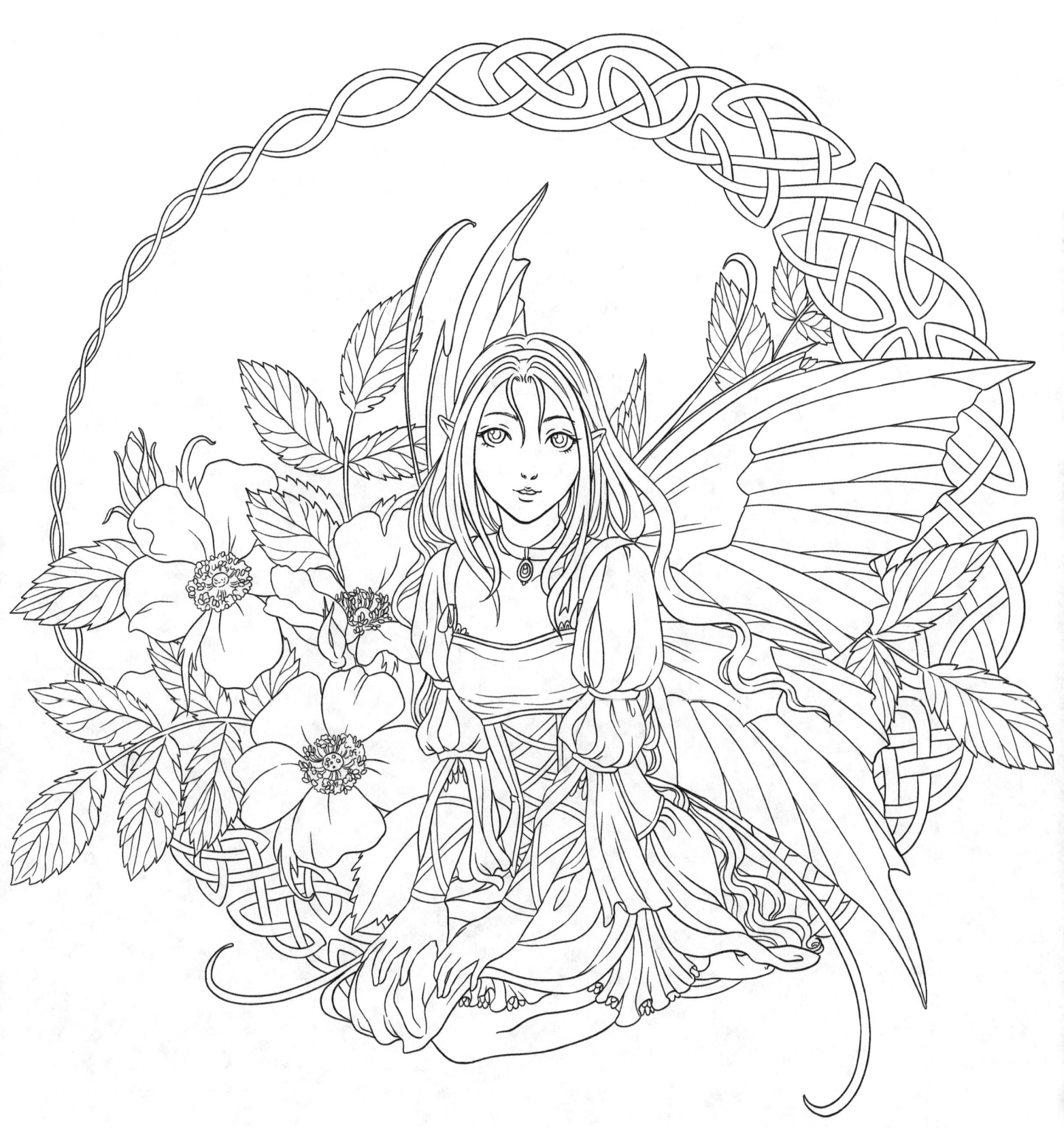

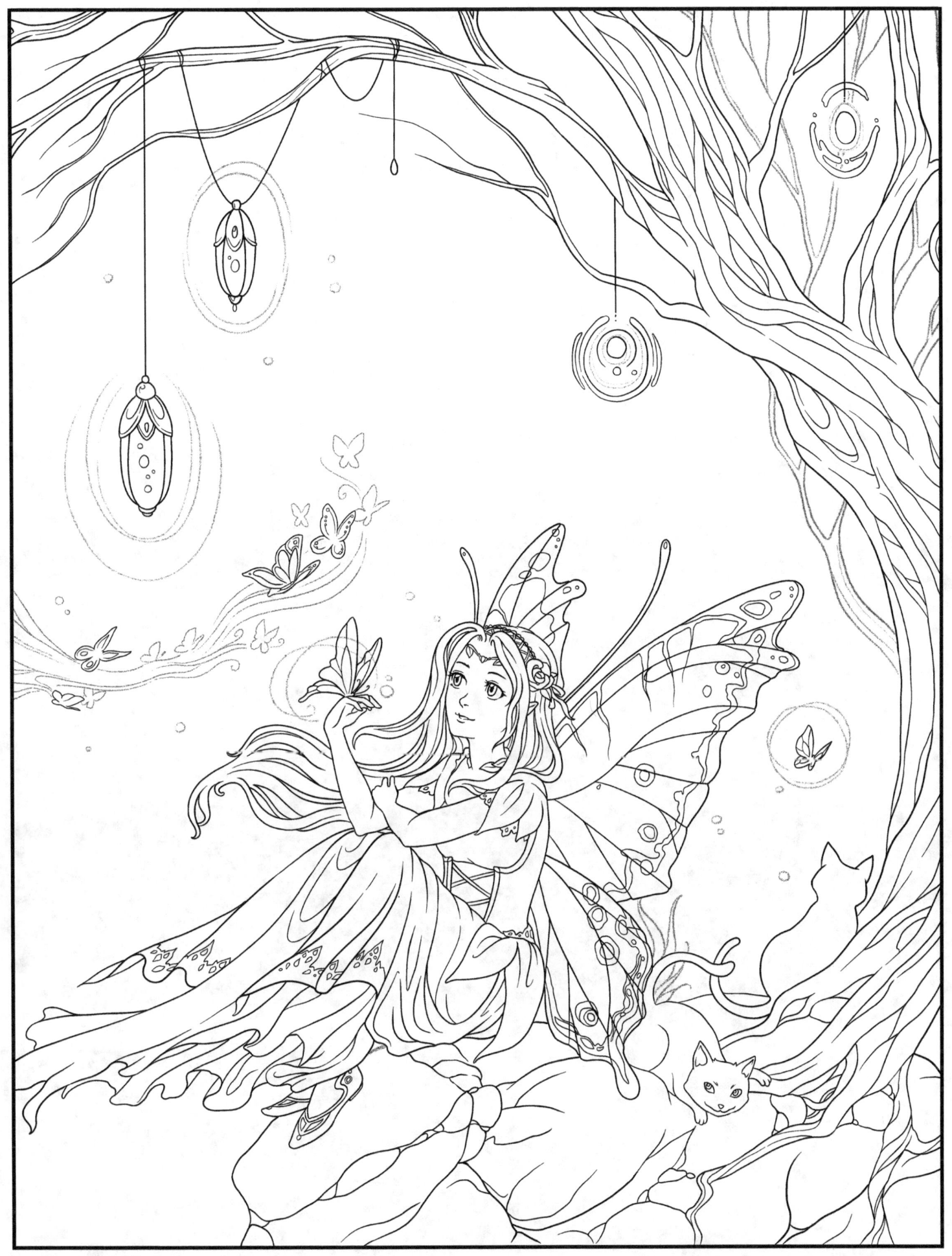

Previous Page: Chasing Butterflies
Lineart by Meredith Dillman

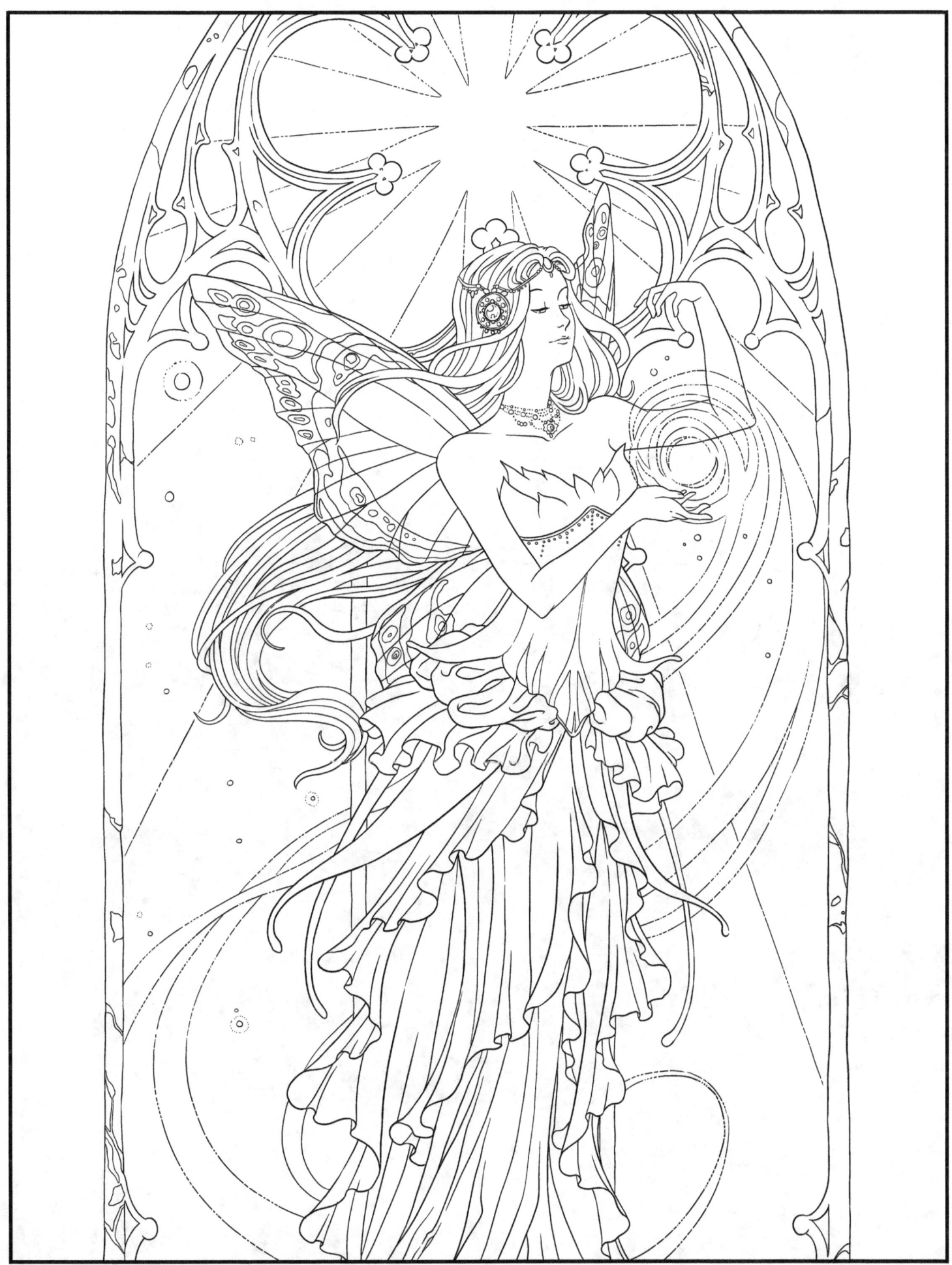

Previous Page: Summer Sun
Lineart by Meredith Dillman

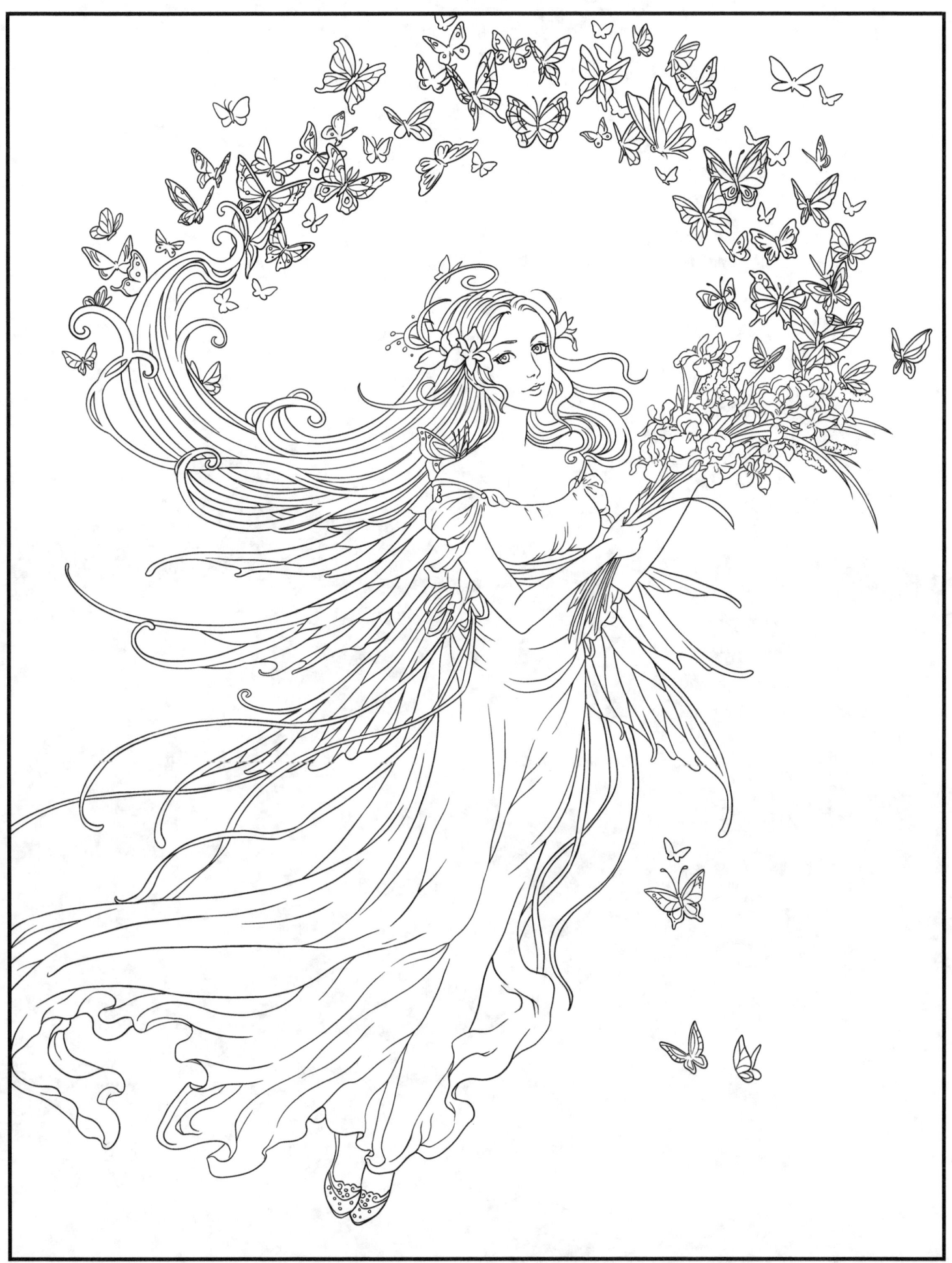

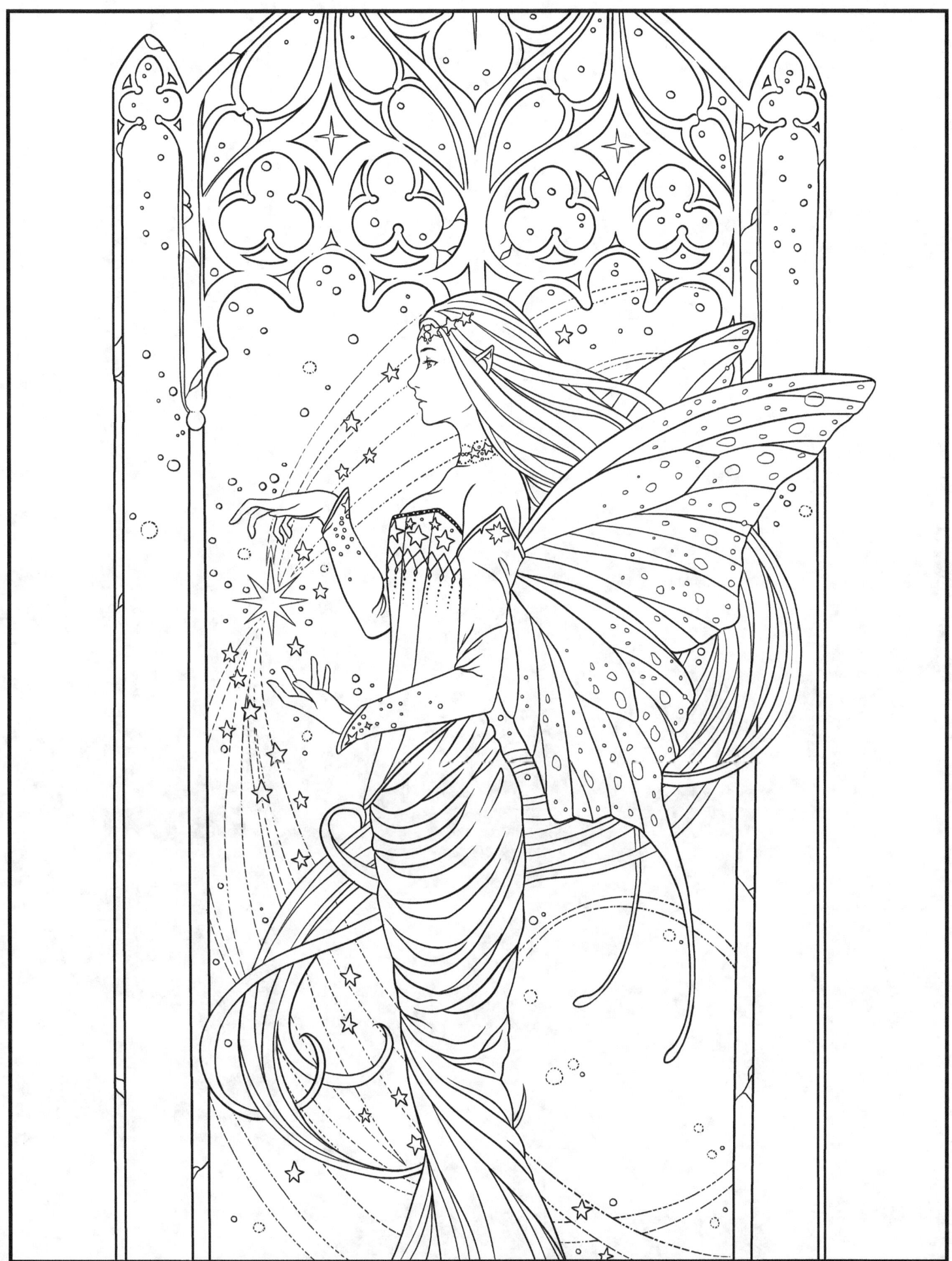

Previous Page: Queen of the Night Sky
Lineart by Meredith Dillman

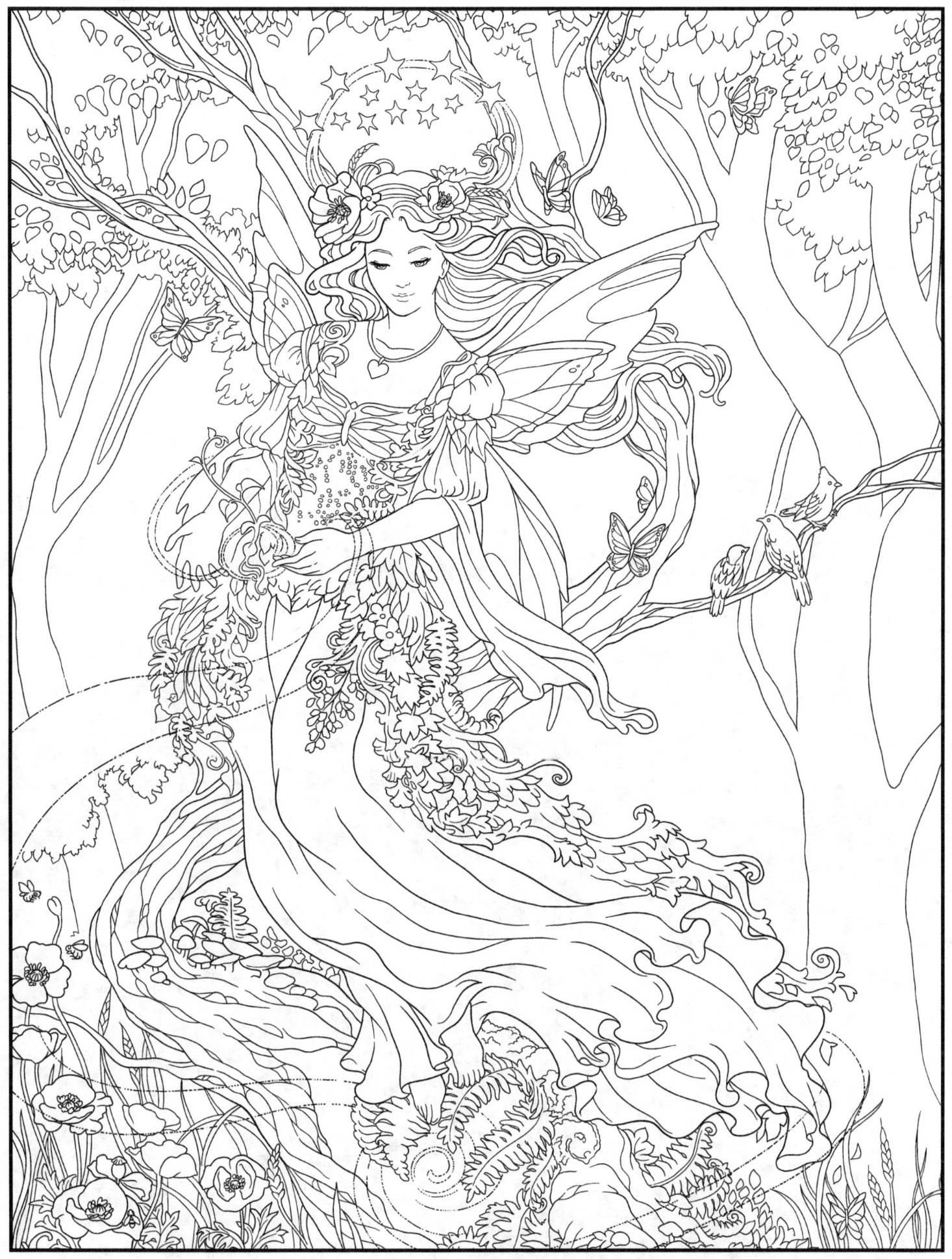

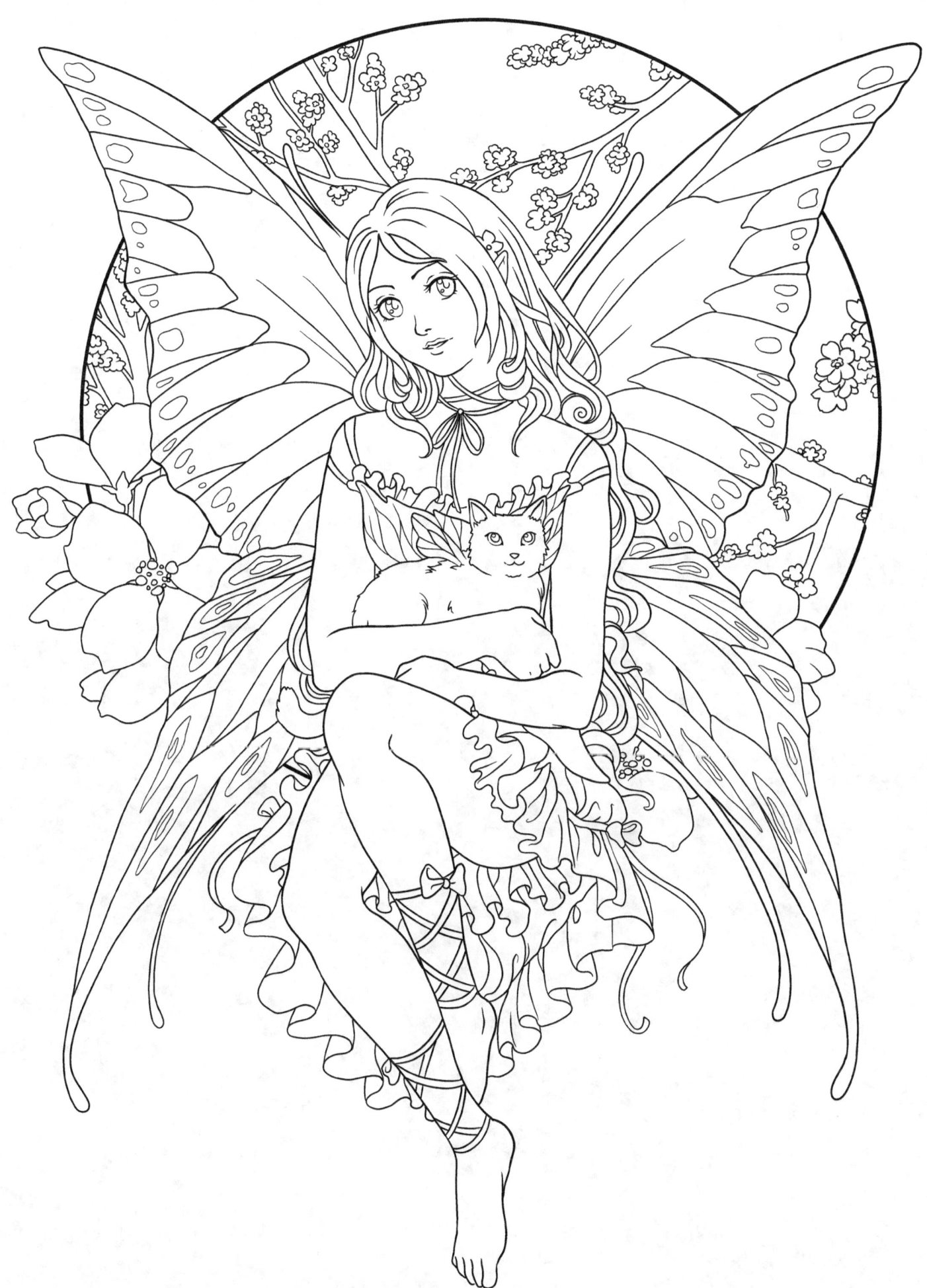

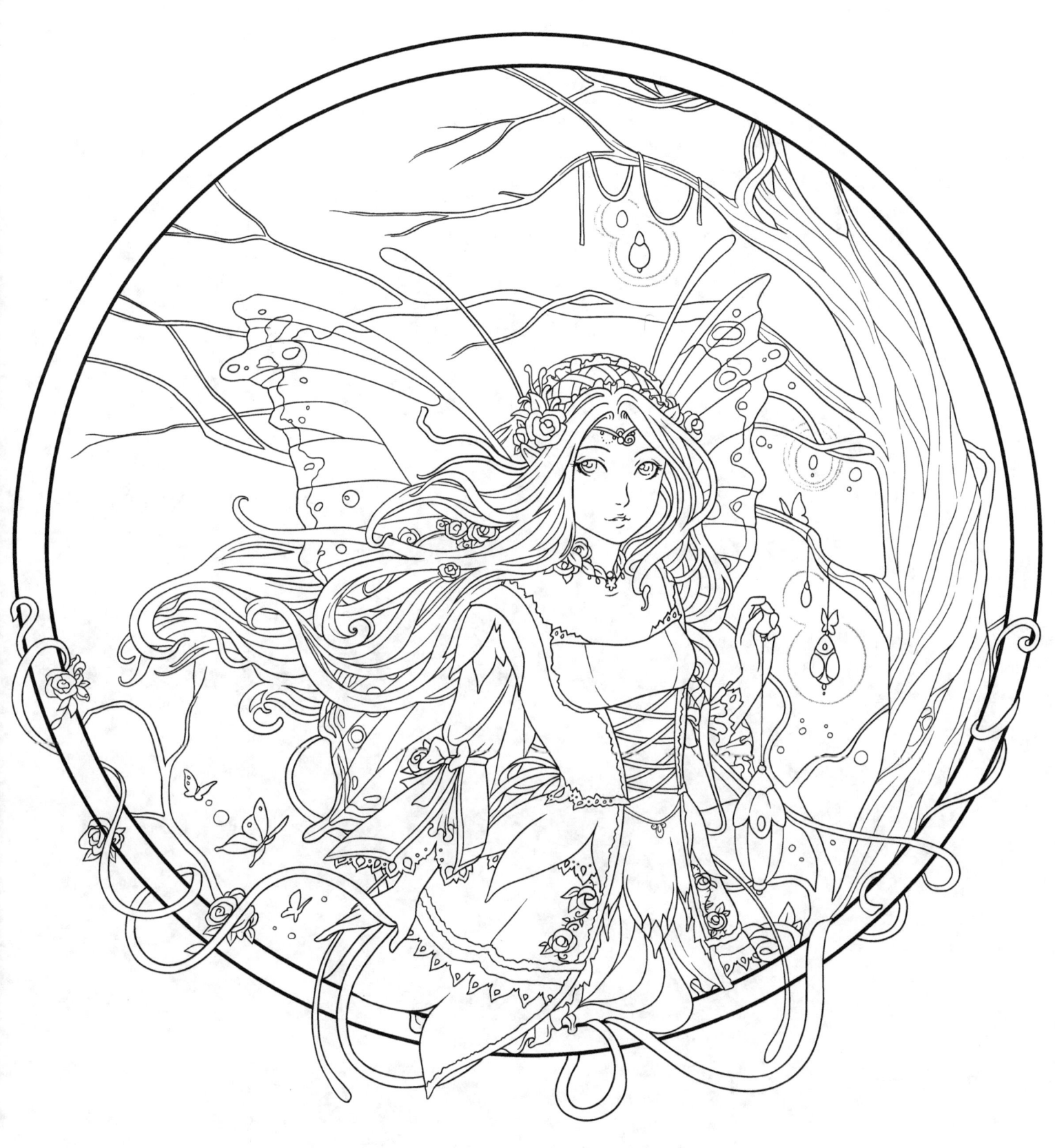

Previous Page: Hanging Fairy Lights
Lineart by Meredith Dillman

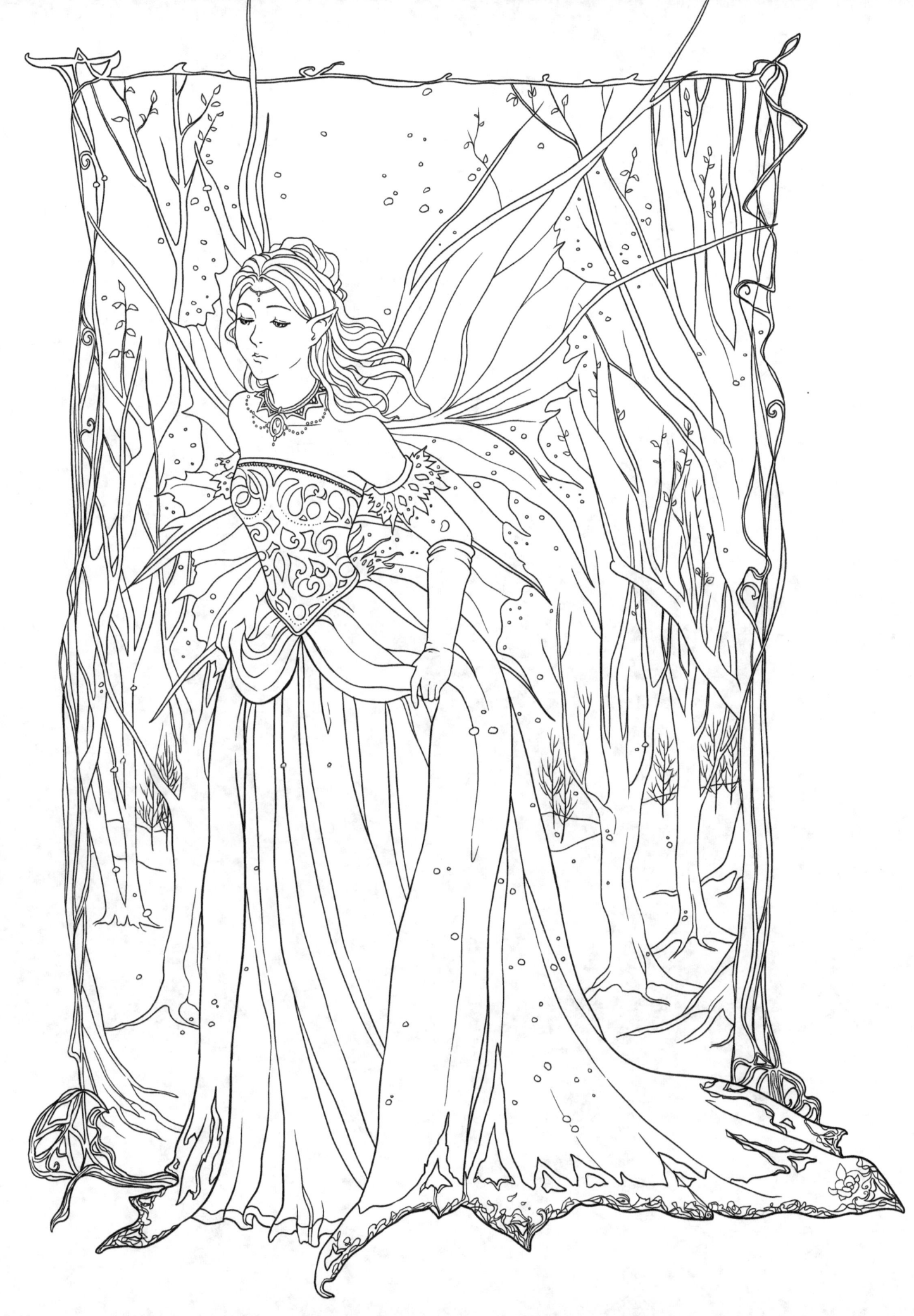

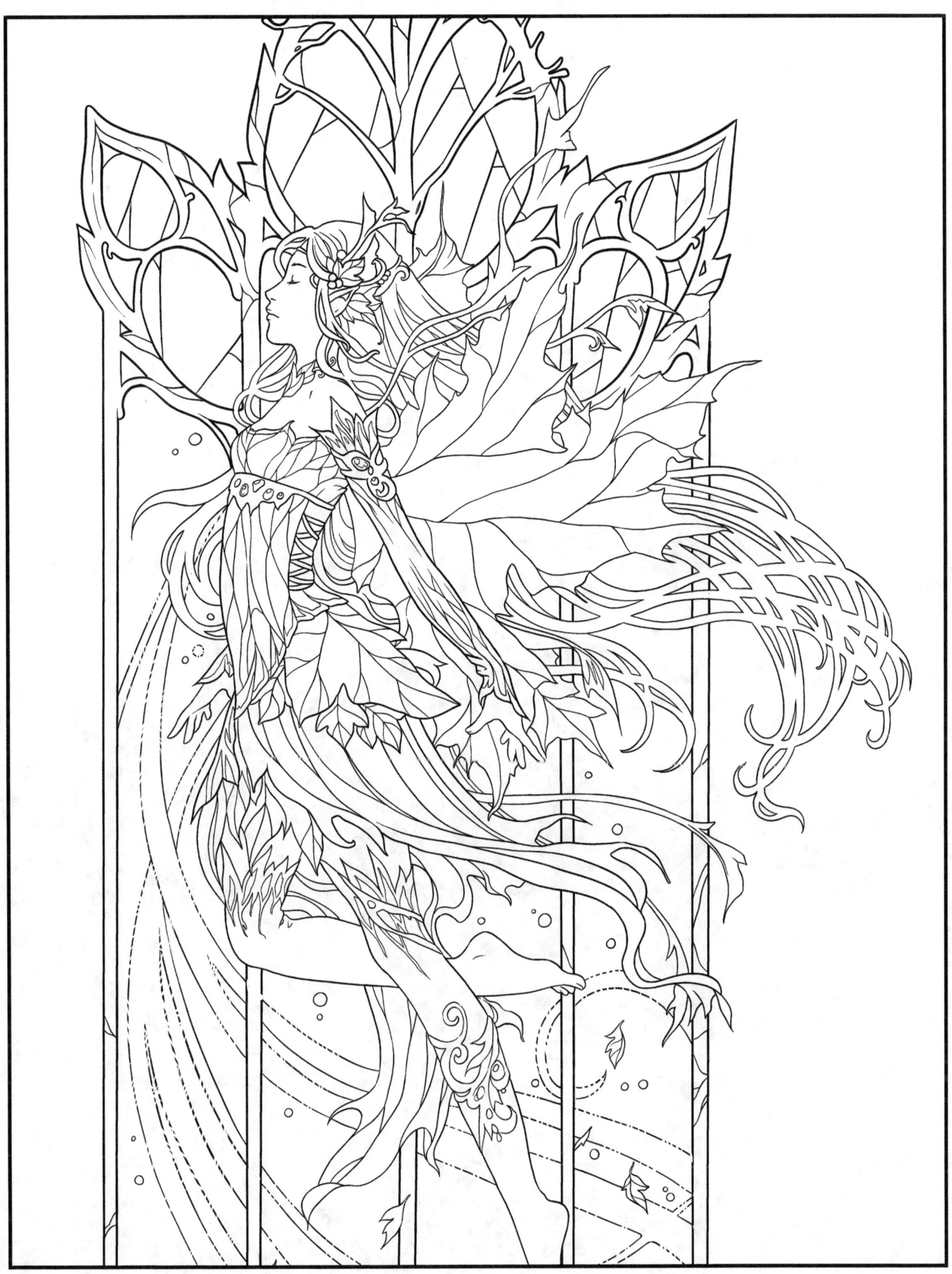

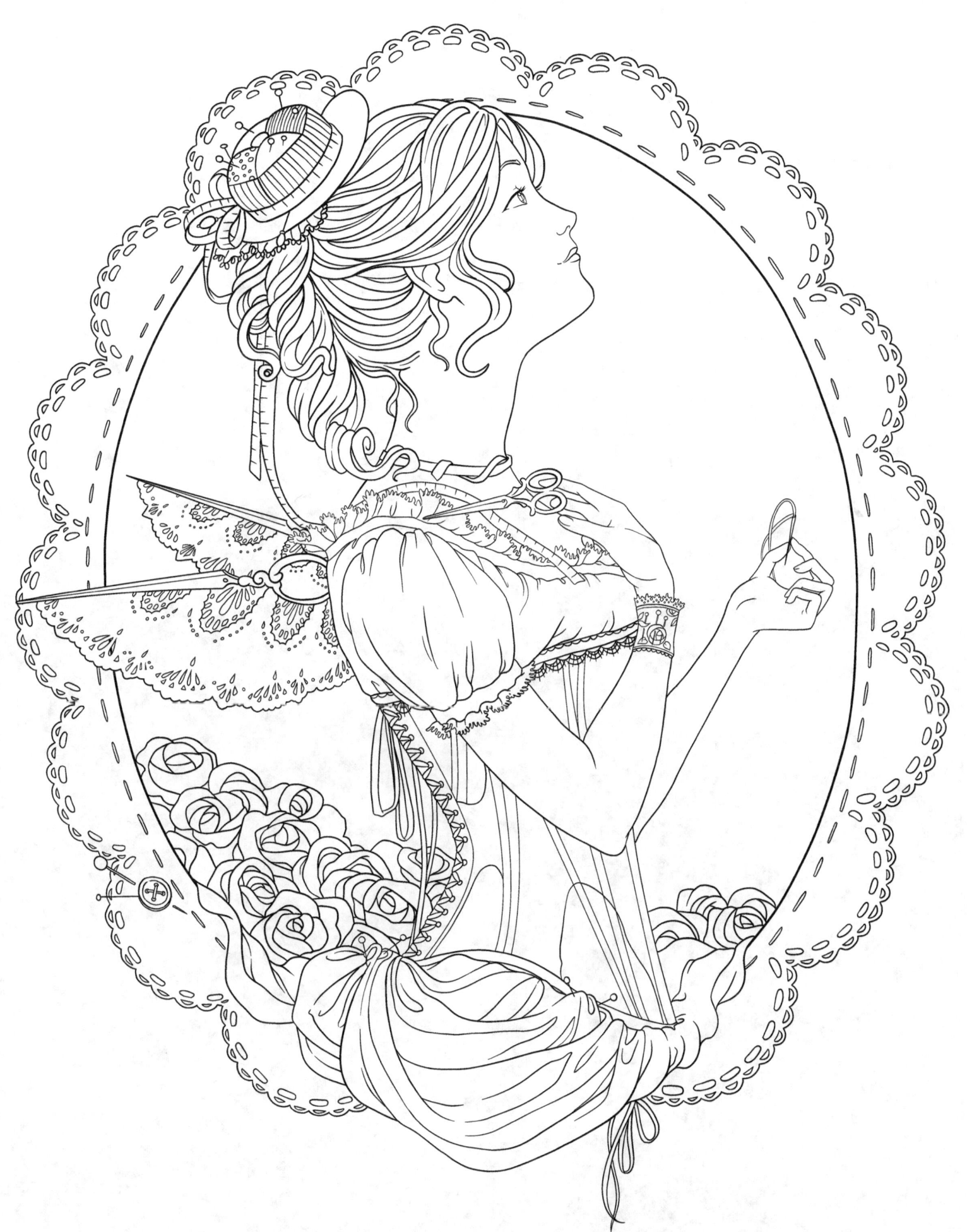

Previous Page: Fanciful Notions
Lineart by Meredith Dillman

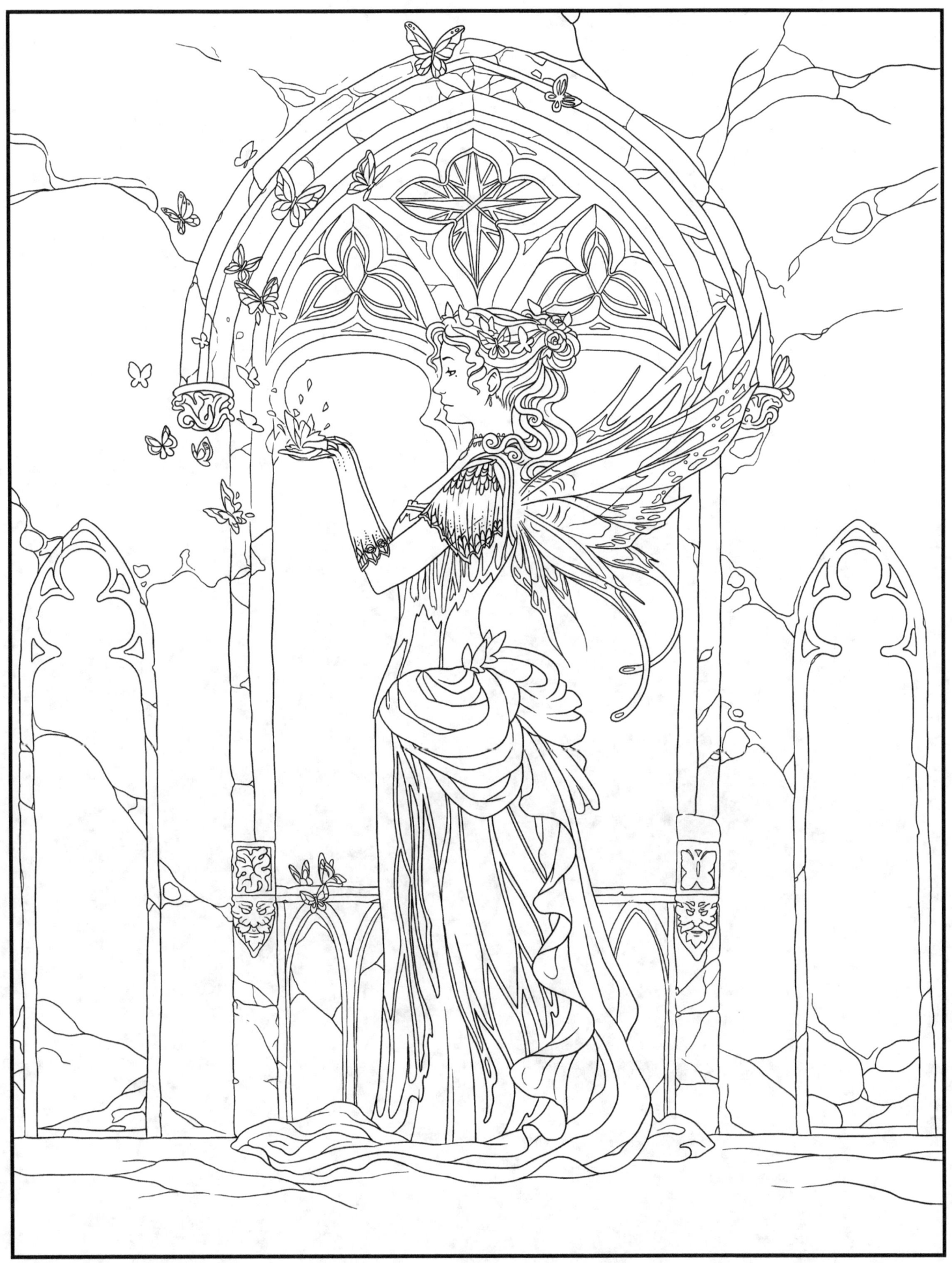

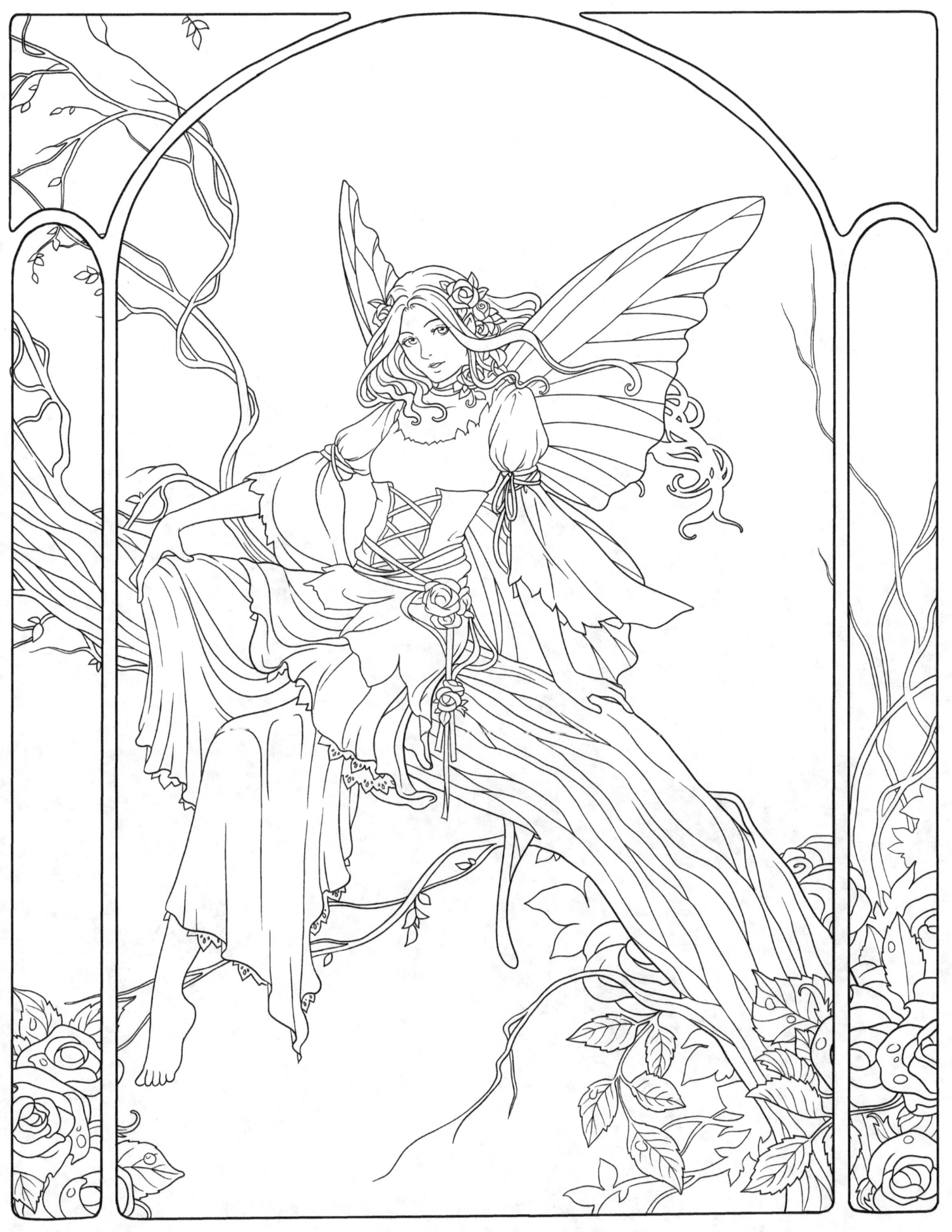

Previous Page: Misty Rose
Lineart by Meredith Dillman

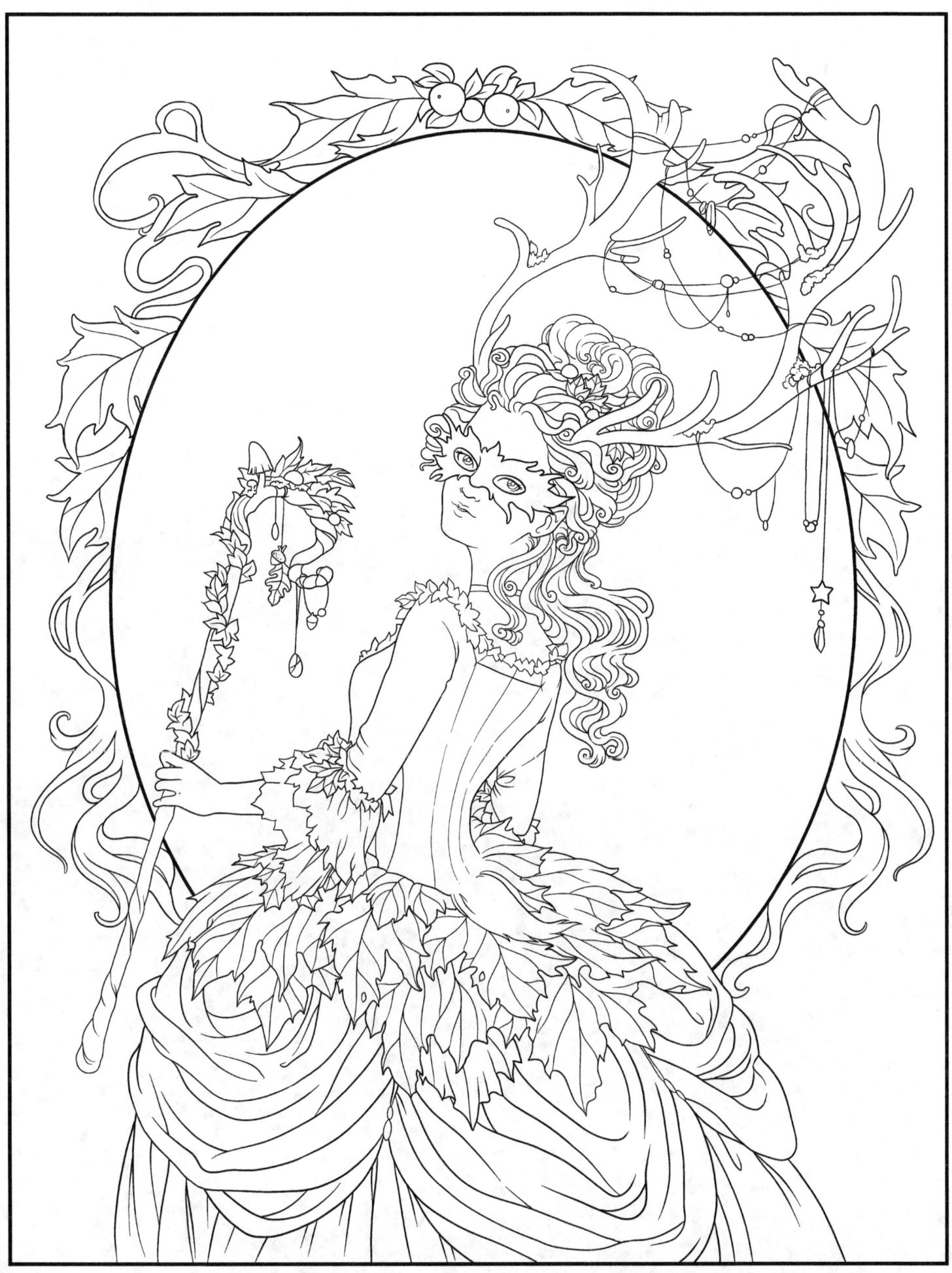

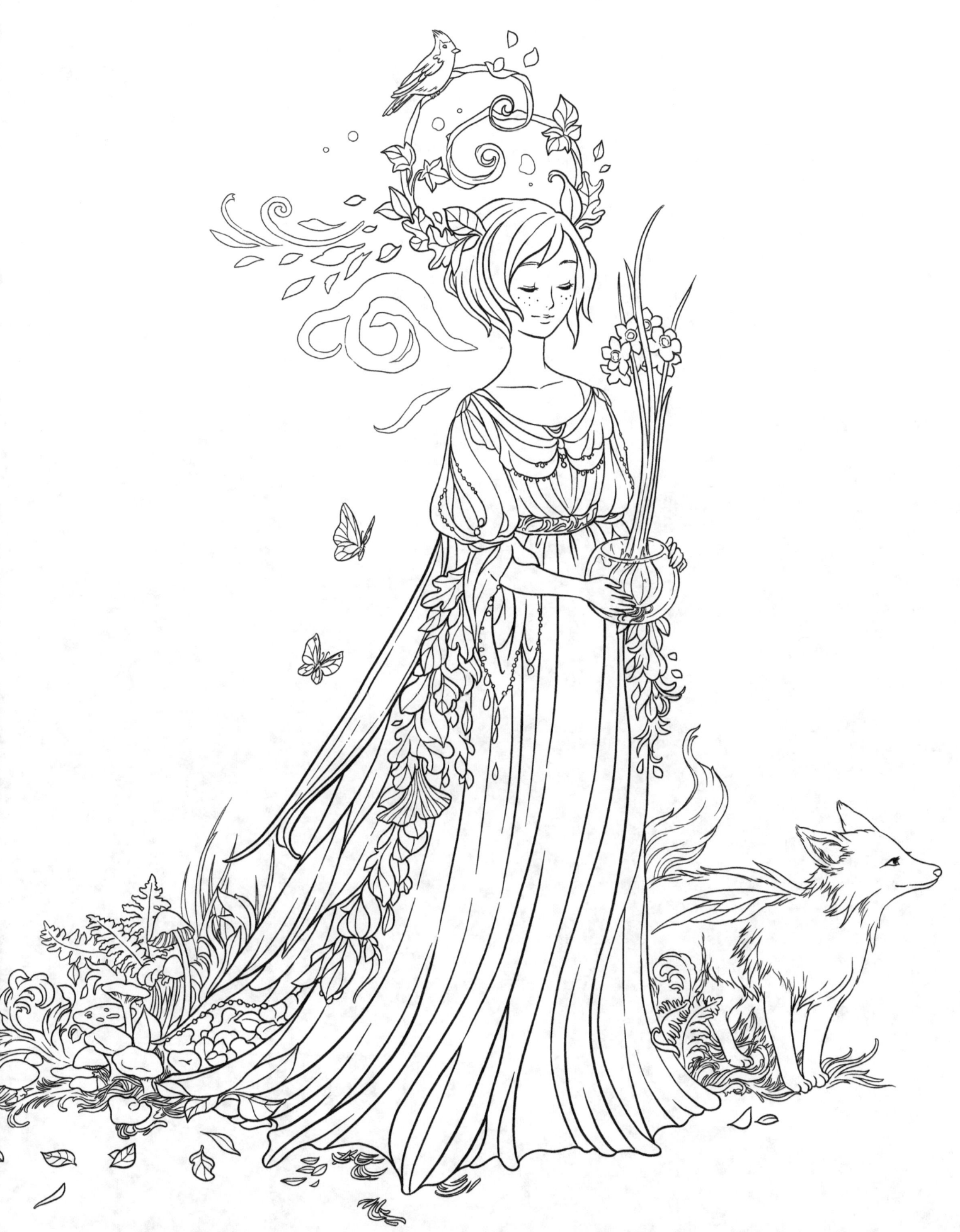

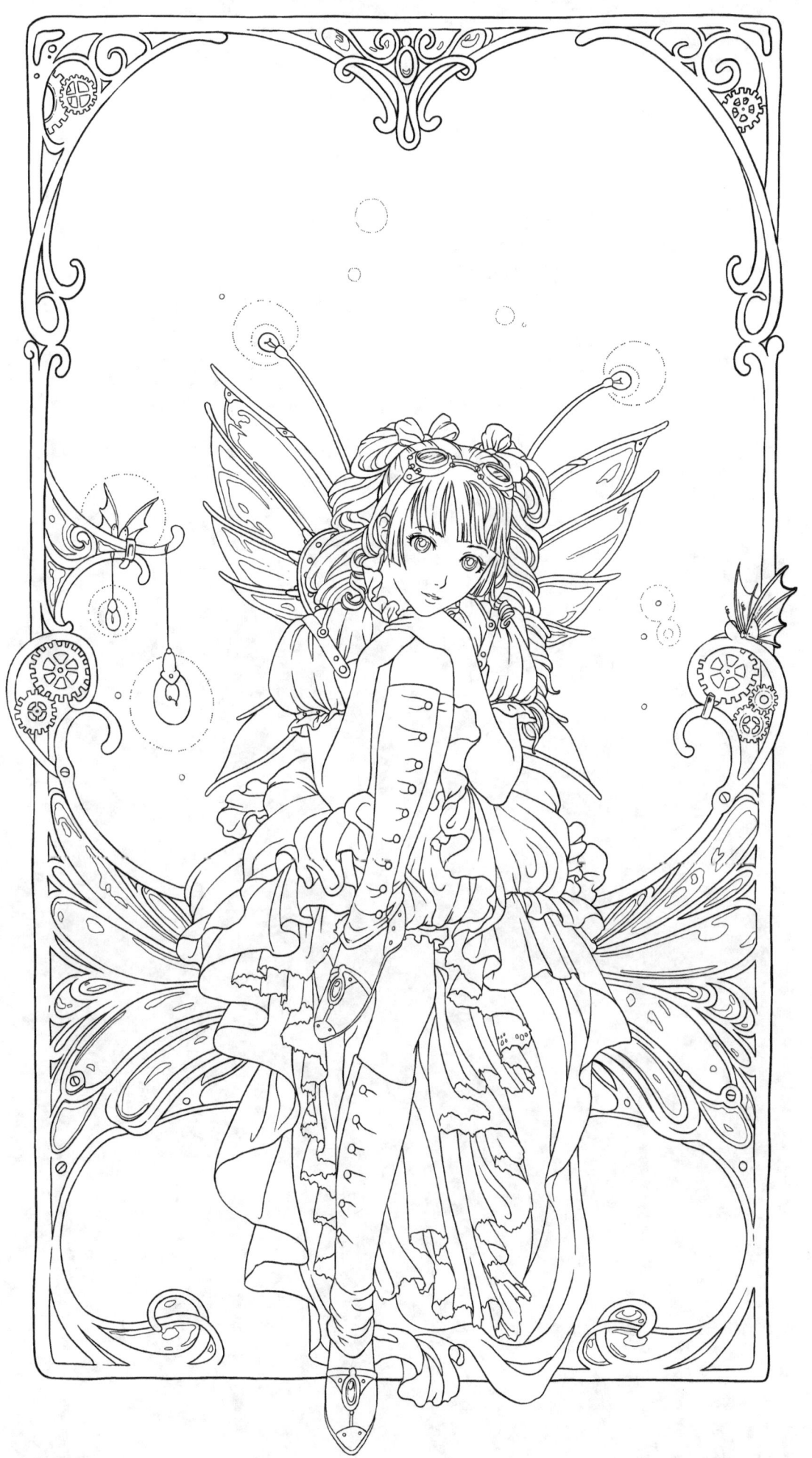

Previous Page: Gears and Glass
Lineart by Meredith Dillman

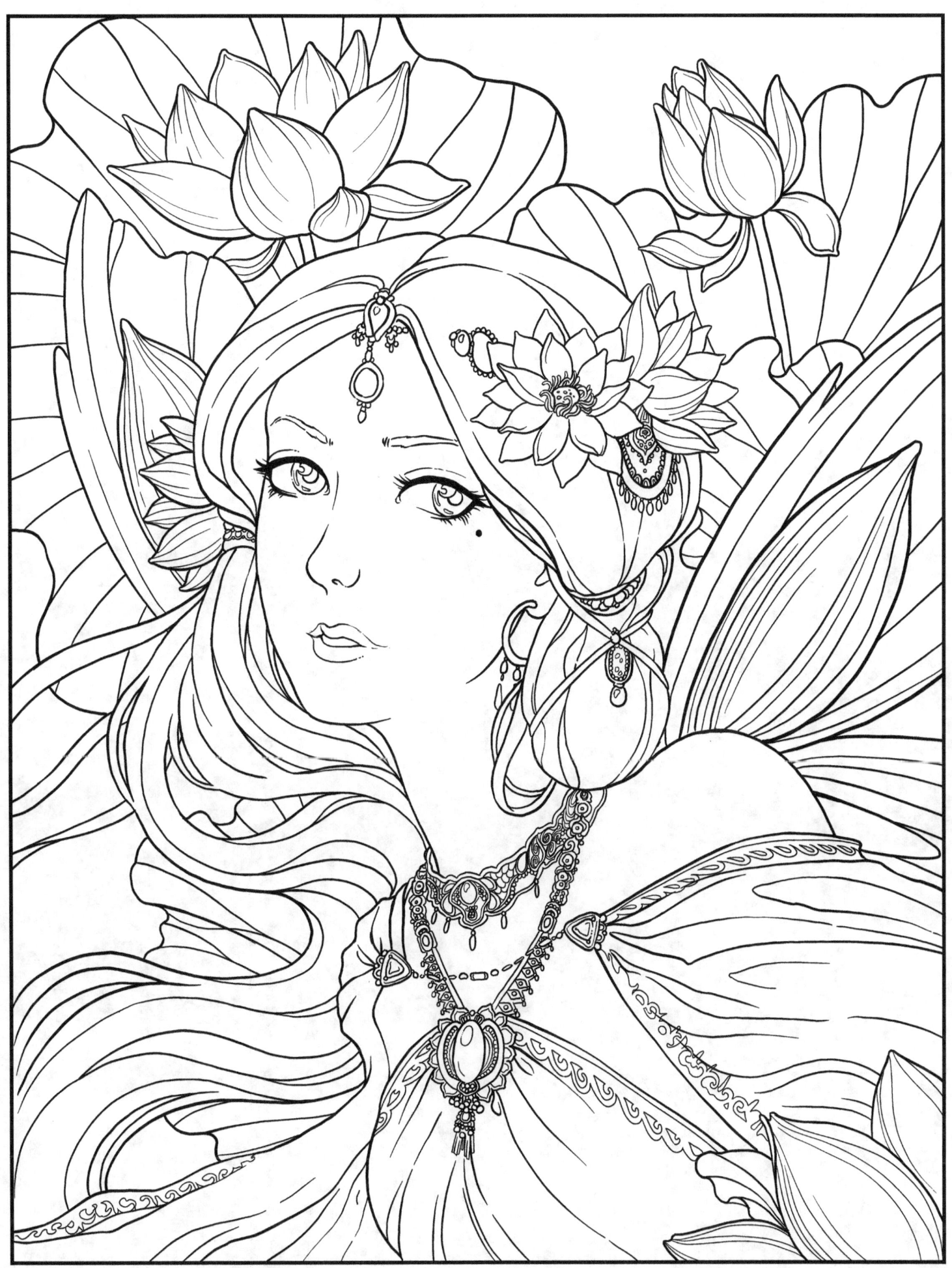

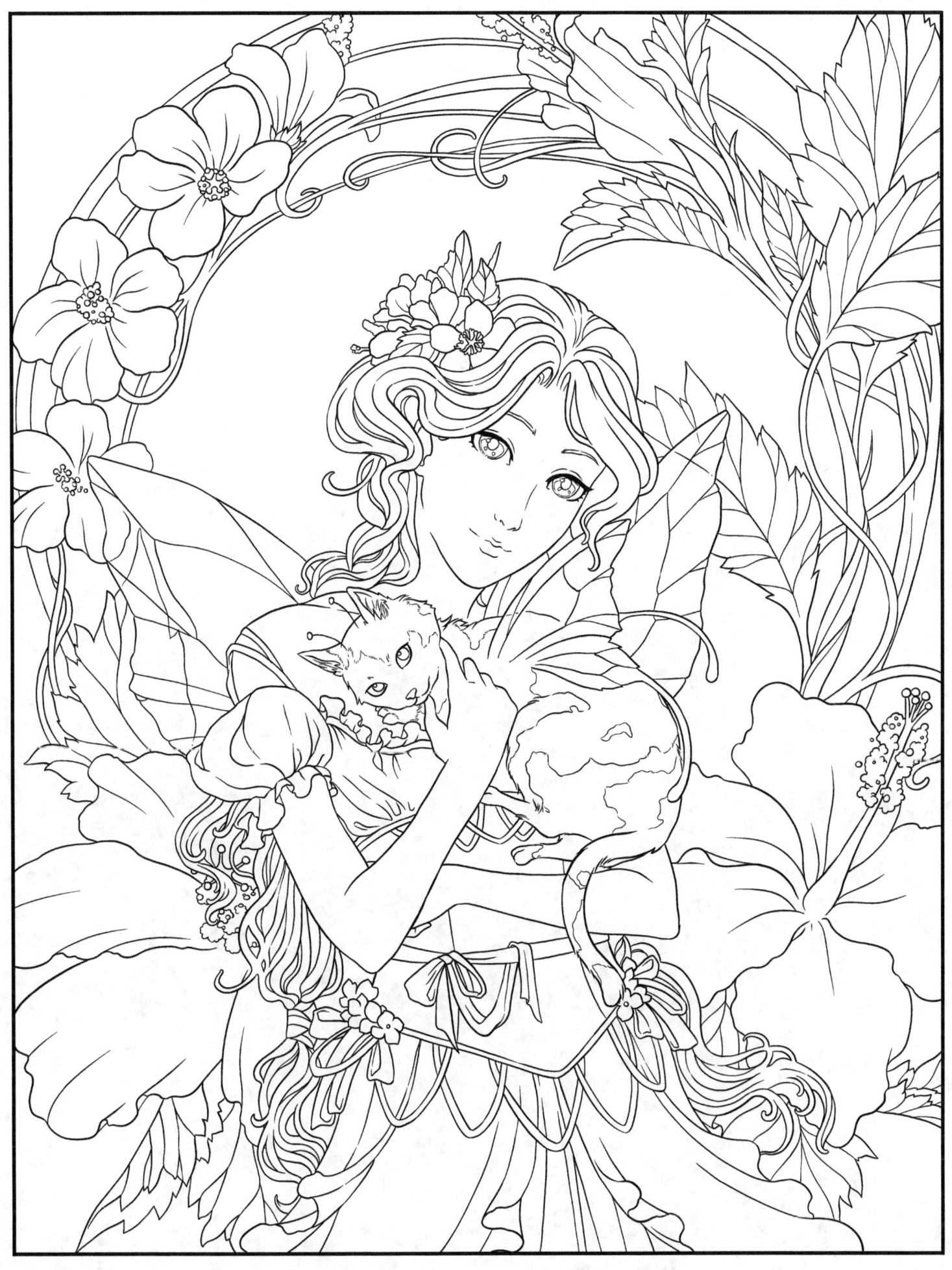

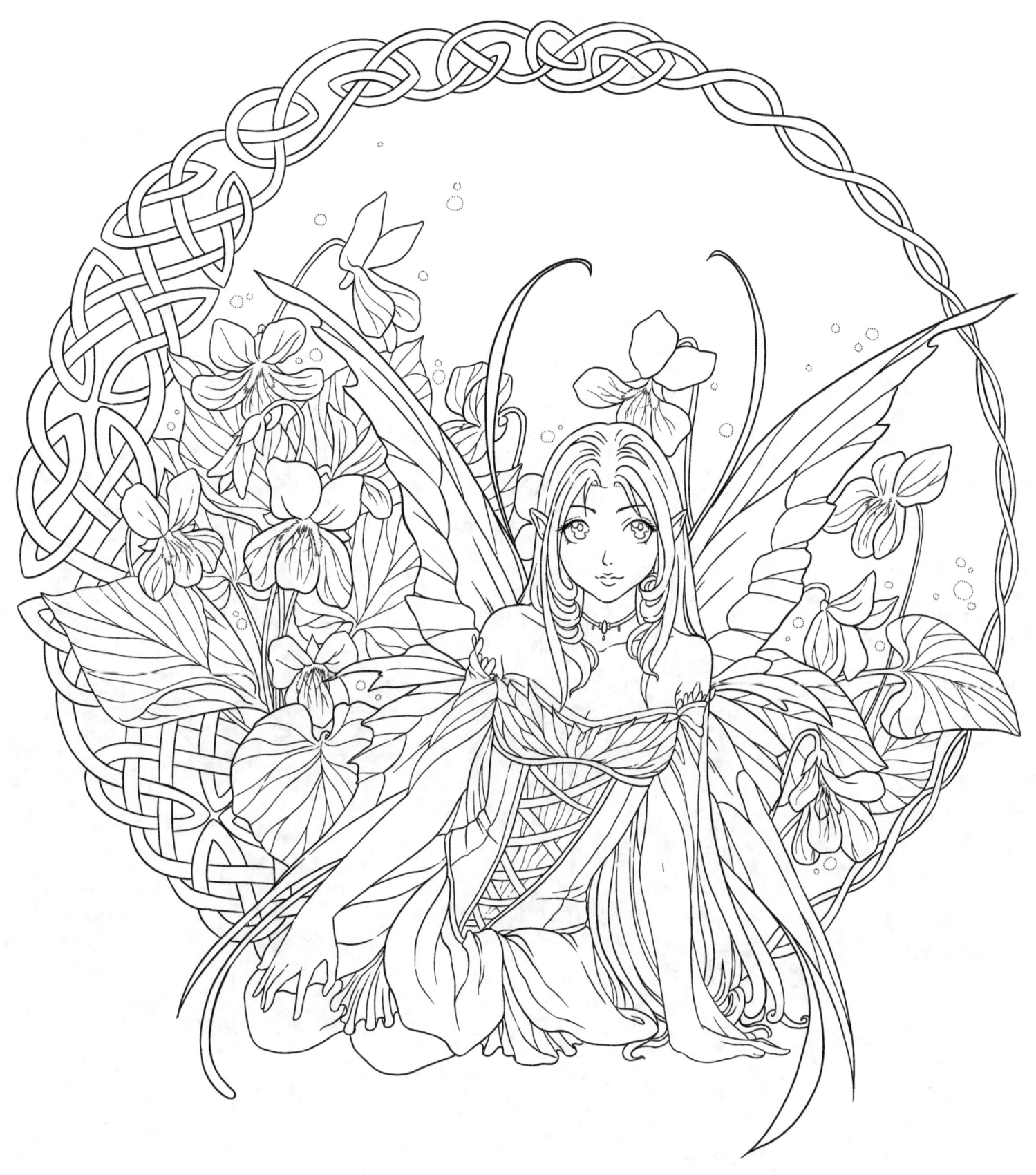

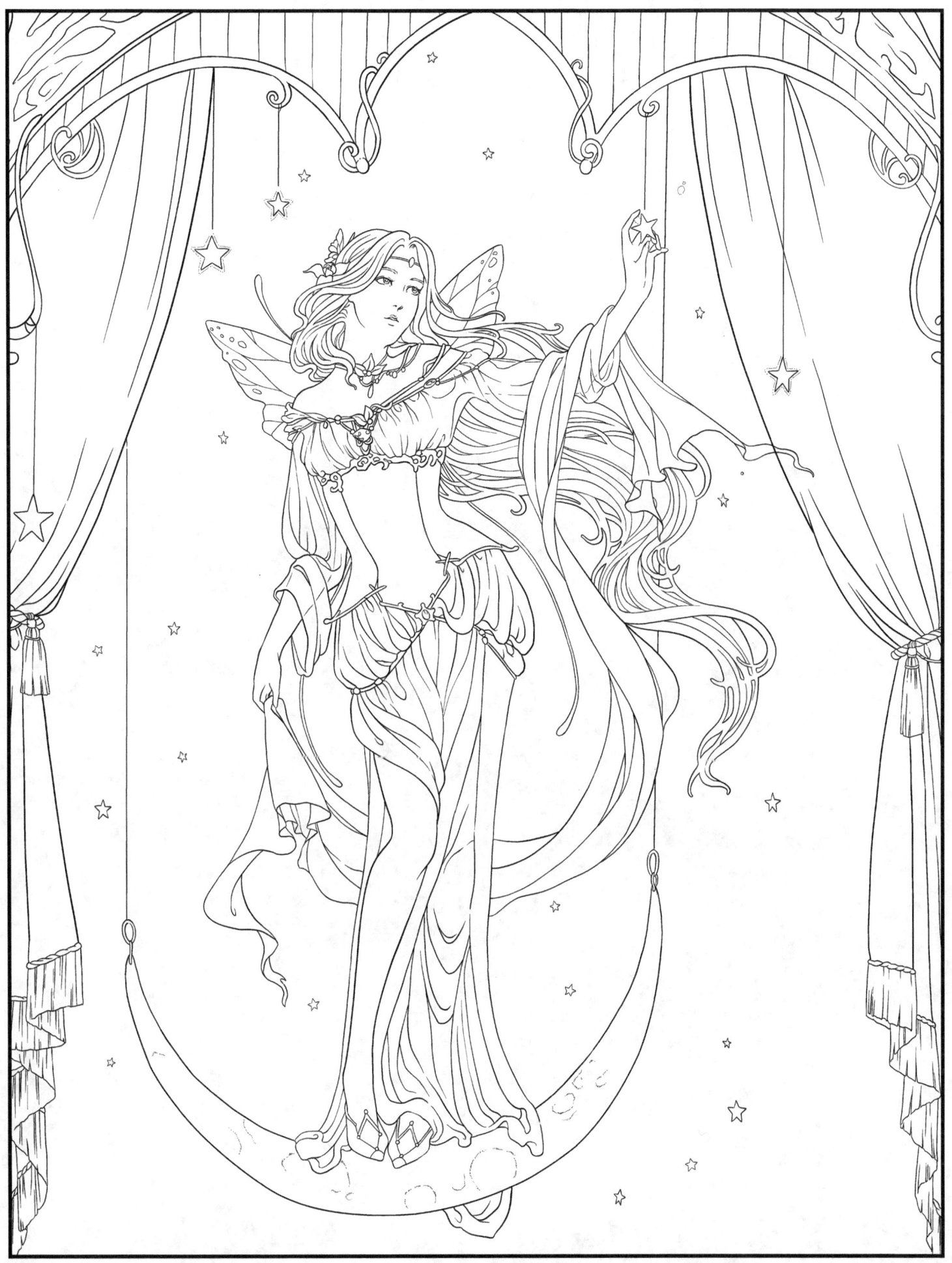

Previous Page: Illura
Lineart by Meredith Dillman

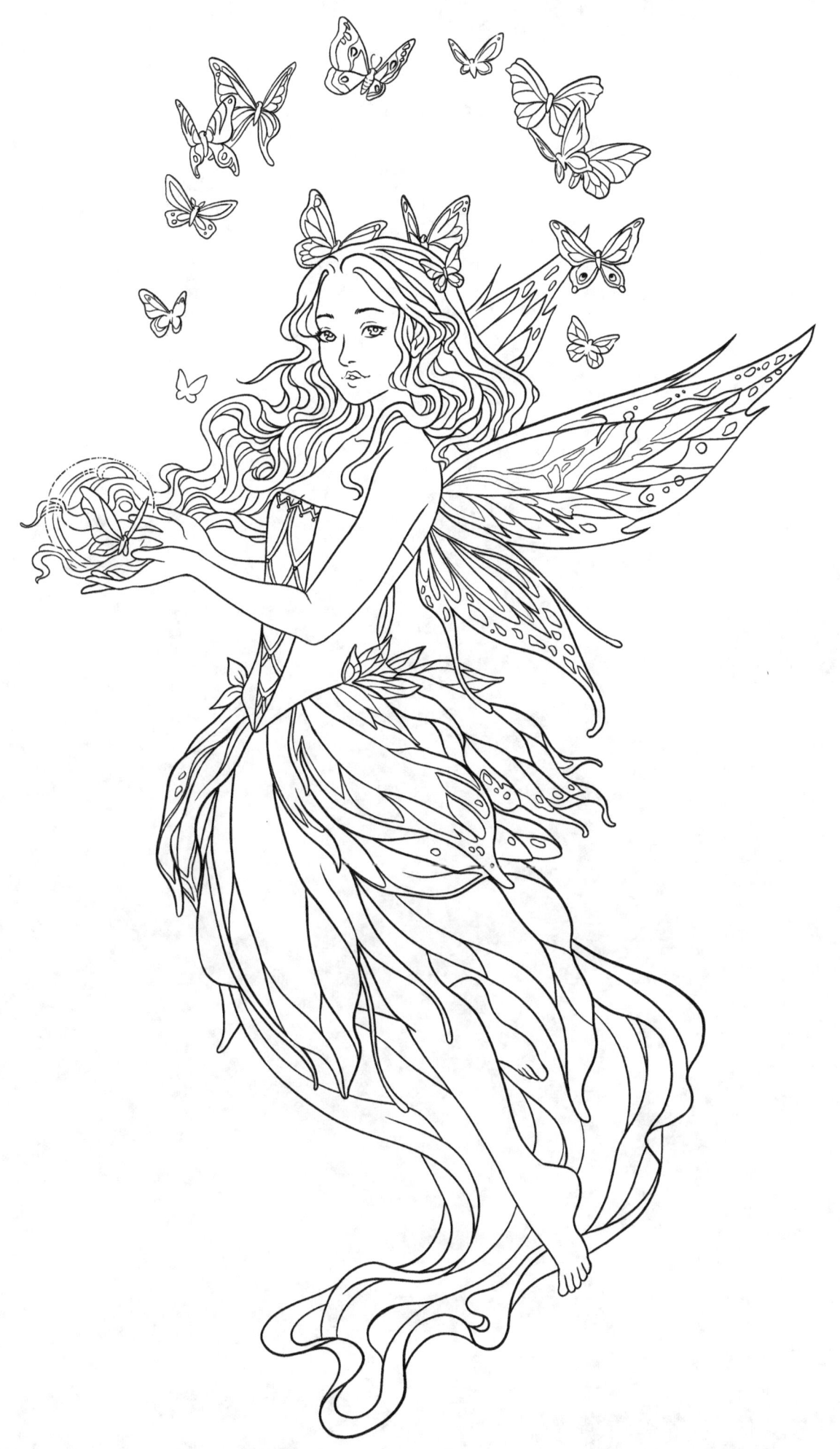